KUNDALINI

AWAK

Achieve Greater Awareness and Turn on Your Inner Light, Open Your Third Eye with Chakra Meditation and Breathing Techniques, Enhance Your Intuition and Psychic Abilities

MIA SCARLETT JONES

Table of Contents

"Observe a child collecting shells on the beach - he is happier than the richest man in the world. What is his secret? That secret is mine too. The child lives in the present moment, enjoys the sun, the salty air of the beach, the wonderful expanse of sand. He is here and now. He doesn't think about the past, he doesn't think about the future. And whatever he does he does it with totality, intensely; he is so absorbed in it that he forgets everything else. The secret of happiness is all here: whatever you do not allow the past to distract your mind and do not allow the future to disturb you."

OSHO

Introduction

As we expand our knowledge of the true world around us, we raise the vibration of ourselves and our planet. We are all connected in the fine fibers of the energies surrounding us, linking our past, present, and future in a harmonious flow. Opening, healing, and balancing the chakras in our body aligns us in unity with this amazing Universe and all that inhabit it. When we see this unity is responsive to our nature to be present and accountable in this life, we are boundless. We stretch our energy across an infinite timeline. Existing in the energy you are in is not limited to your job or the people you surround yourself with. We must supply love to ourselves, healing from past hurt and difficulties that leave us struggling daily. This love can lift others, benefit us enormously, and define our purposes in this great adventure we call life.

In ancient India's spiritual teachings, teaching held that the Kundalini was the meaning inside of everyone that would compel them to grow and evolve in their lives. These teachings have remained steadfast even today, and awakening the Kundalini and using it for one's benefit is the goal of many. This force that lies dormant within you until you call it forth will be the force that will elevate you into a profound consciousness and a profound spirituality. Awakening this power within you is a reality that you can come to know and enjoy in your own life. This reality will change your life in ways you can't begin to imagine. The Kundalini will express itself through you in the form of psychic powers, spiritual knowledge, and ultimate enlightenment. The transformation will bring you to great self-realization.

Life presents many challenges, and each one takes its toll on our physical, mental, emotional, and spiritual well-being. Chakra balancing is a never-ending work in progress, and you will consistently need to check in with yourself to see where you are becoming blocked up or clouded.

The following chapters will discuss the Kundalini and its power and presence in your life. Waiting in a coil at the base of your spine is your Kundalini, the source of infinite energy that is present in all people. You are born with this energy inside of you, and it will die with you. In between birth and death, the Kundalini will wait for you to awaken it and utilize its power to help you realize your full potential physically, mentally, and spiritually.

Remember, this is only the start of what you can achieve, and it is through practice and meditation, you can discover yourself and understand the depths of who you are. There are endless ways to find out your higher truth, so long as you are ready and willing to accept what comes your way.

Chapter 1: History of Kundalini Yoga Philosophy

Since time immemorial, humans have been trying to understand their world and control what is in it. Artists have drawn, sang, and written their interpretation of what the Universe is about. Scientists have sunk a lot of time, energy, and resources into research; religions have risen and fallen, all to uncover the Universe's secret. Yet despite all that effort, every day, something new is discovered.

However, most people forget to look at the most important unit of the Universe themselves in all these efforts. You can't understand the Universe if you do not understand yourself and haven't unlocked all the innate powers that you hold within yourself. Kundalini is one of the most powerful energies of the self. Once locked it allows an individual to understand and experience their world in unimaginable ways. It allows you to exceed your spiritual, intellectual, and physical limits.

The earliest mention of the word Kundalini can be traced to the Vedic writings collected. These writings were referred to as Upanishads, a word used to mean listening to the master's teachings while sitting down. During such lessons, the learners would be given oral recitations of religious insights by a master while sitting down.

During this period, the records point out that Kundalini was an energy science and a divine philosophy. There was no physical component of the Kundalini. However, over time, the Upanishads' position was adopted as the official physical position during yogic activities. It is still in use today. This yoga was never taught to anyone or the public. Kundalini yoga was treated as higher learning for students who had undergone rigorous preparation to equip their bodies and minds for the soul and body instructions from their Kundalini masters.

The choice of a follower who would be taught the science of Kundalini was done in utmost secrecy. This follower had to be from the elite family in addition to possessing particular attributes that set him apart from the rest and which were assessed by the master in secret. Once a worthy candidate was spotted, he would be initiated into the influential Indian Yoga's secret society.

Kundalini awakening was a secret kept from the public. In fact, practitioners thought they were doing the public a favor by not teaching them because; the public was not prepared to handle the power that was to be aroused in them if they knew. Such was the secrecy that covered Kundalini yoga practice.

In the Eleventh Century, the practice extended to Buddhism and Hinduism. Practitioners of these faiths began to experiment in Kundalini awakening with an aim to understanding and unleashing the immense power that lies restrained in the human body. In the Fifteenth Century, practitioners of Hatha yoga began to practice Kundalini awakening. Come the Sixteenth Century, practitioners of Upanishads Yoga began to study and practice Kundalini awakening.

For a long time after that tapping into Kundalini energy remained a preserve of the few, particularly the Chinese and Indians. They guarded it as a great secret that would only be passed from a teacher to a praiseworthy and totally loyal student. Teaching Kundalini or even making known the secret of Kundalini awakening was a taboo and attracted a severe punishment to the perpetrator of such a sin. The practice was deemed as purely religious.

Through their widely practiced yoga, they experimented with the immense power that lay restrained in the human body. These communities had a persistently rich spiritual culture that sought and still seeks to streamline and purify the human body so that it can release Kundalini that is in turn supposed to cause a transformation of the intellect. For the Chinese Taoists, to be ushered into spiritual enlightenment, also referred to as the

Tao, requires that one achieve Yin Yang stability in addition to practicing the microcosmic path.

Between 1875 and 1961, Carl Jung, a psychiatrist, began a campaign to make Western countries aware of Kundalini and the immense power that comes with its awakening. Jung's efforts were largely successful because most of the West's interests in the energy can be traced back to him, as well as other practitioners.

Jung and these other practitioners had experienced Kundalini awakening and had first-hand information of how the energy works. Although its manifestation was different in each of them and their interpretation of the practice of Kundalini awakening was different, they were all working from one common ground; that Kundalini was an energy sleeping in the human being that could be summoned. They also all believed that Kundalini had the ability to advance spiritual development in an individual, but needed to be controlled or mastered well.

These influential practitioners came up with their own proposals on the practice of Kundalini awakening. One of these practitioners, George King, asserted that the entire control of Kundalini through the vertebrae is man's ultimate mission on earth. King also tried to break down the Kundalini awakening process while citing ways in which this can be achieved safely—through living a well-balanced life and devoting oneself to serving people selflessly.

Because of Jung, King and other progressives, the 60s was the decade of progression for Kundalini knowledge. No longer was it a preserve of Easterners. Many Westerners became interested in Kundalini, how to awaken it, and meditation in general. By the 1970s, Kundalini knowledge became even more popular as more people became interested in awakening their innate spiritual and intellectual powers. Driven by this need, more people were trained in awakening Kundalini the correct way as well as recognizing the signs that came with an awakening.

Currently, Kundalini has been adopted and can be mentioned alongside many religious terms or in relation to certain religious organizations, especially the newly launched ones. However, science still remains skeptical of the whole concept of Kundalini awakening, which quite frankly is no surprise since science is more focused on what can be seen, heard, touched, smelled or tasted. Kundalini is more about the sixth sense and what can be felt.

However, despite its skepticism, even science cannot ignore the increased interest in Kundalini awakening, or the changes in people who have experienced it show. Scientists, especially those within the medical field, have been studying Kundalini to understand how it can be applied to therapy and healing. Some medical practitioners have inculcated Kundalini yoga into their routine procedures and practice it in their clinics. A lot of research has also gone into determining the link between mental stability and meditation.

The problem with this haphazard integration of Kundalini into medical therapy is that rarely are the correct awakening procedures followed. When this happens, side-effects to those being incorrectly prepared and awakened can be disastrous. There have been cases of patients suffering from mental and emotional disturbances. Therefore, some medical personnel have taken this to mean that Kundalini, in general, is a dangerous practice that shouldn't be tried out.

Fortunately, as the practice of Kundalini awakening grows, more and more information about Kundalini awakening is being disseminated to the public. The issue is that most of the disseminated information speaks to what the awakening is but does not go deeper into the issue, explaining the step-by-step process of awakening or what to do afterward. You're in luck because, in this guide, I've tried to explain these steps as well as how to do them safely.

Chapter 2: What Is Kundalini Yoga, and What Are its Goals

Kundalini yoga is a specific yoga practice designed to awaken, balance, and harmonize Kundalini energy. Individuals who embark on a Kundalini yoga journey often report that they begin experiencing the awakening symptoms after just one or two sessions. This awakening furthers as they move deeper into their Kundalini yoga journey. This yoga form also helps support the Kundalini energy, keeping it awakened, complete, and thriving in the individual practicing it.

Kundalini Yoga

Not all yoga practices are done equally. Some are designed to stretch out the physical body, some are designed to facilitate a mind-body-spirit connection, and others are designed for specific purposes, such as Kundalini yoga.

Kundalini yoga does not emphasize the physical as much as other practices, such as Hatha yoga. Instead, it incorporates meditation and mantras as a foundational part of the overall practice. The combined experience of the mind, body, and spirit being brought together through these three practices encourages Kundalini awakening and supports Kundalini flow. The body is supported and awakened by the yoga poses, the mind is supported and awakened by the mantras, and the spirit is supported and awakened through meditation.

Introduced by Yogi Bhajan in the 1970s, Kundalini yoga is still relatively new to the Western regions. It is, however, rising in popularity as more individuals seek to incorporate the mind, body, and spirit connection in their lives.

The Bodies

There are ten bodies associated with Kundalini yoga. All ten bodies are awakened through Kundalini yoga, allowing individuals to begin to continue feeling full Kundalini flow. These bodies are as follows.

The Soul Body

The soul body is your flow of spirit. This is where you connect to your Soul and to infinity. The soul body is considered to be the foundational body and your true self. It provides you with the ability to live from your heart. This body responds to any form of heart work, as well as the raising of your Kundalini energy.

The Negative Mind

Your second body is your negative mind. This is one of our strongest bodies, as it consistently works toward assessing the environment and circumstances you are in and if there is any danger present as a result. This body is responsible for your ability to stay alive and gifts us with what is often called "a longing for belonging," which is a phrase coined by Yogi Bhajan. Your negative mind can be balanced through integrity and discipline.

The Positive Mind

The third body you have is your positive mind. This works toward assessing what is positive, beneficial, and affirming in your environment and circumstances. This body allows you to see where opportunities lie and where you may be able to access resources. The playful mind is responsible for bringing willpower and playfulness into your life. Everything you do with your navel point, or your core, contributes to your positive mind. You can also balance it by increasing your self-esteem.

The Neutral Mind

Your neutral mind is responsible for guiding you through assessing the information coming in from both your negative and positive minds. The neutral mind is compassionate, recognizes polarities, and works on intuition. The neutral mind can be balanced through meditation, which is a foundational part of Kundalini yoga.

The Physical Body

Your physical body is your temple. This is where all of the other nine bodies come together to exist in harmony. This body allows you to be able to balance yourself and your life. You can also sacrifice for your hopes, dreams, and the greater community through your physical body. The physical body possesses the energy of the teacher. It is balanced through regular exercise. The physical body also loves to share what has been learned with others.

The Arcline

Your arcline body is like a halo that wraps around your head around your earlobes, brow, and hairline. If you are a woman, you have a second arcline that exists across your breast line. Your acrline body allows you to intuit the world around you, as well as project yourself upon it. You can use this body to help you focus and meditate. Any practices associated with the pituitary gland or the third eye (pineal gland) support the arcline body's awakening.

The Aura

Your aura body is your electromagnetic field of energy that extends around the physical body. It is responsible for holding your life force energy and shielding you and providing protection. Through your aura body, you can elevate yourself both energetically and consciously. Natural fibers are worn on the body as well as meditation both contribute to awakening and balancing your aura. You can also incorporate the color white into your life and practice, which is believed to magnify and expand your aura.

The Pranic Body

Your pranic body is supported by your breath, which brings life force energy into your physical body. This allows you to experience accomplishment and energy in your life. You interact with this body every time you breathe in and out. The pranic body is awakened and supported by pranayama practices.

The Subtle Body

Your ninth body is your subtle body, and it is responsible for helping you see beyond the physical matter and into what else exists. This body is deeply connected to your soul body, as it carries your soul body after your physical body dies. Many wonderful teachers and gurus continue to teach us through their subtle bodies despite no longer being in the physical realization. Your ability to master anything exists within this body. If you want to experience mastery, do a Kundalini practice for 1,000 days in a row. Then, your subtle body will be balanced.

The Radiant Body

Your tenth and final body is your radiant body. This body is responsible for giving you radiance, courage, and nobility. When you meet someone who is naturally charismatic and magnetic, they have a balanced, radiant body. To balance and awaken your radiant body, you need to have commitment. Through the art of being committed to your practice, truth, kindness, and excellence, your balance and awaken your radiant body.

Embodiment

Though not technically a body itself, the embodiment is an important element of awakening the 10 bodies. Embodiment suggests that all ten bodies are awakened and balanced. This is the ultimate goal with Kundalini. When you practice Kundalini yoga, you are awakening, balancing, and strengthening your ten bodies.

Yoga Poses to Awaken the Bodies

The following yoga poses are written in the sequence in which they should be completed. There are 14 poses in total, all of which are designed to help you awaken your Kundalini and your 10 bodies. You must remain mindful of your breathing and use each of these as a pose to meditate in. You can also repeat a mantra to help you further integrate your mind, body, and spirit.

Easy Pose

Easy pose, known as Sukhasana, is the first pose you are going to start with. This pose requires you to sit on the ground with your legs crossed and bringing your hands in front of your heart. Bringing the hands in front of the heart in this way is known as the prayer mudra. Rub your palms together a few times, warming them up. Then, relax your thumb joints into your sternum.

Stretch Pose

Gently move from easy pose down to your back, with your legs stretched straight below you and your arms straight down by your sides. When you are ready, bring your heels together and point your toes away from your body. Gently lift your head about 6 inches off of the ground and look down toward your toes. If this feels like it is too much or like it is bringing discomfort, you can slide your hands under your lower back and use them to support you. As you do this, practice the breath of fire (explained below.) Hold this sequence for about 1–3 minutes. If you are pregnant, do not practice this pose or the breath of fire.

The breath of fire is pranayama. To do it, you want to inhale while pushing your navel away from your spine, then exhale, pulling your navel back toward your spine. This allows you to fill your diaphragm, lungs, and throat with air and then exhale all of the air from your throat, lungs, and diaphragm.

Knees to Chest Tuck

While laying on your back, after you finish the stretch pose, you can move into a knees-to-chest tuck. Simply bring your knees up, wrap your hands around them, and then gently pull them toward your chest. If you are feeling confident, you can lift your head up. Your nose should be pointing between your knees. Use the breath of fire and hold this position for about 1–3 minutes. If you are pregnant or are experiencing a heavy menstrual cycle, you should substitute the breath of fire of long deep breathing. Breathe in for about six seconds and out for about six seconds. Do not hold your breath at any point.

Ego Eradicator

When you are done with your knees to chest tuck, you want to come back up to a seated position with your legs crossed in front of you. Begin creating the easy pose by bringing your hands back into the prayer mudra in front of your chest. Then, curl your fingers in and point your thumb up toward the air, as if you are giving someone two thumbs up. Your fingers should only be lightly curled, with the fingertips gently touching the palms and the majority of the palms remaining exposed. Then, put your hands up above your head and out to the sides. This opens and exposes your chest and core. Close your eyes and practice the breath of fire for about 1–3 minutes before moving into the next pose. Again, if you are pregnant, refrain from using the breath of fire and instead practice deep breathing.

Hold Your Toes

Now, you want to uncurl your legs and stretch them out to the sides in front of you. Your legs should be spread in a wide "V" shape in front of you. Keep your feet flexed with your toes pulled back toward your body. Do not push yourself to stretch further than is comfortable in this pose. Allow yourself to relax into it and trust that the more you practice, the more flexible you will become and the easier this pose will get. When you are ready, take a deep inhale and stretch your arms over your head. Then exhale and stretch your hands out to your feet, holding onto your toes and relaxing into the pose. Hold this for about 1–3 minutes.

Grasp Your Shins

Cross your legs once more, returning to an easy pose. Hold each of your shins. Then, inhale and flex your spine forward, curling it over as if to expose your back. When you exhale, flex your spine backward as if to expose your chest. You should be getting a good relaxed stretch out of this, so keep it calm and intentional. Do this pose for between 1–3 minutes before moving on to the rock pose.

Rock Pose

To complete the rock pose, you will need to tuck your feet under yourself and sit on your shins with your knees together in front of you. You should be sitting on your heels with your feet relaxed. Let your hands gently come to a resting position on your thighs before flexing the spine as you were in the previous pose. Your eyes should be closed and gently rolled toward your third eye if you feel comfortable doing this. Continue this stretching pose for about 1–3 minutes.

Grasp Your Shoulders

Remain in the same seated pose as you used for rock pose, with your heels underneath you. Keep your torso and head pointed forward, looking directly in front of you. When you are ready, lift your arms up and gently grasp your shoulders with your hands. Your left thumb should be behind your left shoulder with your fingers rested above your left collarbone. Likewise, your right thumb should be behind your right shoulder with your fingers rested above your right collarbone. Sit in this stretch pose for a few moments. Then, on each inhales, twist toward the left, and on each exhale, twist toward the right. Your arms should remain lifted, keeping your biceps parallel to the floor during this pose. Do this for 1–3 minutes.

To take this pose a step further, stay in this posture, return your torso, and head to center, looking directly in front of you. Your hands should remain in the same position, with your elbows extended out toward the side. Each time you inhale, lift your elbows up, drawing a line toward the sky. When you exhale, draw your elbows down, returning to your original position with your biceps parallel to the floor. Do this stretching pose for about 1–3 minutes.

Shoulder Lifts

Take a few moments to return to a crossed leg position. Then, gently rest your hands on your knees and allow them to relax completely. Refrain from drawing your knees up in this position, as these shoulder lifts can sometimes result in tight hips causing your knees to draw up toward the sky. Allow them to relax toward the floor instead. When you are ready, inhale and lift the left shoulder toward the sky. As you exhale, lower the left shoulder and simultaneously lift the right shoulder. Continue this for 1 minute before reversing the process. As you reverse it, lift your right shoulder on the inhale, and drop it to lift your left shoulder on the exhale. Continue the stretch on this side for another 1 minute.

Double Shoulder Lifts

After completing your alternating shoulder lifts, you can begin lifting both shoulders at the same time. For this, you want to lift them and try to pull them toward each other on the inhale. Then, drop them and push them away from each other, allowing them to relax on the exhale. Continue doing this double shoulder lift practice for 1 minute.

Turn Your Head

As you continue to hold the easy pose with your legs crossed in front of you and your hands rested gently on your knees, you can begin turning your head. This will stretch out your neck, upper spine, and upper back area, allowing you to experience a pleasant, relaxing sensation. Each time you inhale, turn your head to the left. When you exhale, turn your head to the right. Your head should remain level, and your nose should draw a line around your head that is parallel to the floor. After you have done this for one minute, reverse the breath. On each inhalation, turn your head to the right, and on the exhalation, draw your nose across the front of you, turning your head toward the left. When you are done with this reversed breathing part of the pose, bring your head to come back to a resting position in front of you, slowly exhale, and relax your body.

Frog Pose

This will be one of the more advanced poses of the yoga session. The frog pose requires you to come up into a squatting position, resting on your toes. Your heels should be drawn up toward the sky and touching each other beneath you. Your fingertips can be placed on the ground between your knees, with your fingers separated wide and each tip firmly planted into the ground. Evenly displace the weight between each of your fingers and toes to allow for a centered pose. Your head should be lifted with your chin pointing upward, allowing you to gaze toward the sky. Don't lift your head too hard, but rather allow for a nice relaxed upward focus. As you inhale, stretch your legs out slightly allowing your glutes to rise toward the sky. Remain on your toes for this pose. As you exhale, come down to the original position. Continue holding this rhythm with your breath for about 54 repetitions. However, if this is beyond your skill level, you can always aim for 13 to 26 repetitions. Continue adding more to your practice each time until you reach the 54 repetition mark.

Laya Yoga Meditation

With most of your poses now completed, you can enter the meditation part of the process. Here, you want to sit back into the easy pose — Left your wrists to rest on your knees as you point your palms toward the sky. Then, bring the tip of your thumb to the tip of your index finger and create a circular shape. This is called the Gyan mudra. Now, chant the following mantra. As you are chanting, take the time to visualize energy that spirals from your spine's base to the top of your head. This is the realized energy of Kundalini.

The chant is as follows:

- "Ek Ong Karah,
- Saa Taa Naa Maah
- Siree Whaah, Hay Guroo."

You want to continue chanting and meditating for a total of 11 minutes to experience the full effect of this process. Carry the visualization from the base of your spine to the top of your head during the entire process, allowing it to unfold naturally in whatever way it manifests for you. Refrain from forcing the energy, but rather set the intention and allow it to show you how it wants to be realized, rather than the other way around. This is an excellent opportunity to explore the practice of releasing blocks by allowing the process to unfold.

Savasana

Lastly, you want to end your Kundalini yoga sequence with a savasana pose. This pose requires you to gently lie down on your back, with your feet down and gently separated and your arms relaxed out to your sides.

Breathe intentionally but with a natural rhythm here and relax as the energies flow through your body. Instead of trying to create or force anything, receive all that comes your way. This will allow you to integrate the entire yoga experience. You can gently guide your awareness between the ten bodies, balance, and wholeness from this pose.

Chapter 3: What Is Kundalini and What It Wakens

In the previous chapter, you were given a glimpse of what Kundalini Awakening can be. This chapter is dedicated entirely to Kundalini Awakening. You will learn what it is, what methods are used to awaken it (both spontaneously and consciously), the symptoms that you are likely to experience, and what it feels like.

So, to reiterate, Kundalini is the female creative energy lying latent (in the form of a coiled snake) at the base of the spine in every one of us. However, there is no physical evidence of the presence of this snake-like element in our bodies. It is a subtle energy form you have the power to awaken and know its presence when you experience its power.

Like prana and the nadis or channels through which it flows, Kundalini is invisible to the human eye but can be felt and experienced when it is in its active state. This subtle form of energy contains other elements of our non-physical self, including our energetic imprints, natural and acquired patterns of energies, and emotional imprints. Kundalini is the place where our life experiences, including the ones created by our family, culture, and society (collectively called "samskara" in Sanskrit).

Interestingly, although the energy contained in our Kundalini appears metaphorical, or even metaphysical to novices, you can rest assured that it is not. Kundalini is subtle but definitely does exist and is something that many of us are capable of activating and awakening using a variety of methods, including meditation, yoga and others.

You can feel the Kundalini energy the same way you can feel your skin or see something colorful through your eyes. You can feel Kundalini energy dance up and down through your spine and the nadis in your body in the awakened state. As it moves freely, you can also feel the dissolution of all the energy blockages in your body. As the different blockages of energy accumulated over the years are released, your insight into long-held beliefs is improved, and you can see things in a clearer form than before.

Most experts are bound to agree that awakening the Kundalini without guru guidance can be dangerous, both for you and the people around you.

Kundalini awakening can happen either through the conscious practice of yoga, meditation, and other techniques and a result of trauma, near-death experience, a debilitating illness, in dreams, misuse, and abuse of drugs or even by having sex with a partner with an awakened Kundalini. Awakening the Kundalini requires unprecedented levels of the firm discipline of our body and mind so we can be ready to accept the responsibilities that accompany the power of waking up the innate Kundalini.

So, why should anyone try to awaken the Kundalini Shakti? Ultimately awakening the Kundalini journeys back to God, or the universal divine power. It helps to get rid of your ego, too, as you surrender yourself to the universal divinity. The final purpose of Kundalini awakening is for self-realization.

Yes, the awakening of Kundalini might seem like a crazy experience that could lead you to situations beyond human control. Yet, that is only a part of the process. Kundalini is, in reality, an organic and intelligent process with a systematic purpose at the end.

An awakened Kundalini helps you untie all the emotional and mental knots in your mind so that you can see the true purpose of your life, in particular, and the Universe, in general. The awakening of the Kundalini is the rising of Shakti within you. It also means the path for Shiva to enter you is getting cleared and ready.

Kundalini awakening means Shakti is calling out to Shiva to come down and meet Her even as She climbs up to meet Him. Kundalini Awakening is an exercise to bring divinity into our materialistic world more than trying to transcend our life. Kundalini Awakening is a process of purifying our body, mind, and soul so we become containers ready to receive and hold the universal divine power within us.

Kundalini Awakening is frequently seen as a divine revelation as it comes with a multitude of mystical experiences like connectedness with the entire Universe, bliss, beautiful colors and lights, and perception of beyond-human planes of consciousness. The truth, interestingly, is that Kundalini Awakening is nothing more than the first step of a long journey back to where you come from. When you wake up the dormant, sleeping Shakti, the real work is just about to begin.

If you have gone through spiritual healing and purification, then it would be a smooth and not-so-difficult transition that happens when the Kundalini awakens. However, if the Shakti awakens before you are ready or in a hurry, the experience can be quite unpleasant.

Effectively, when the Kundalini awakens, it is like waking up a sleeping giant or giantess, in this case. She will purify your body, heart, and mind. However, if you have the Kundalini before dealing with the problems and other unpleasant aspects of your life, then the "cleansing" process can hit you hard. Therefore, you mustn't force the awakening of the Kundalini. Let Her wake up in Her own time when She knows you are ready to accept Her in the active state.

The process of purification needed before the Kundalini Shakti is woken up can be difficult and intense. You might need to be hospitalized or even institutionalized, as it can be quite disorienting to live in the materialistic world with a fully awakened Kundalini. Once She wakes up, then your world will never be the same.

Therefore, if you are keen on awakening the Kundalini Shakti lying latent in you, then make sure you truly understand its potential impact. Understand how deep your desires are, and know that the path will not be easy. Finally, remind yourself that you could face a situation where you wish you hadn't woken HER up if you do awaken the Kundalini.

Awakening the Kundalini Shakti is not just about psychic powers and bliss and oneness with the Universe. It is also the hard work involved in the spiritual path. However, once SHE is awake, she is in control, and you can only do what you have to do. So, decide after thoroughly thinking things through.

Chapter 4: Kundalini Yoga the Supreme Knowledge

Kundalini Yoga is one of the schools of yoga that focuses on awakening Kundalini energy in a person's body by practicing asanas (postures), pranayama (breathing techniques), meditation, and chanting of mantras. It seeks to nurture and cultivate human beings' spiritual potential and their innate ability to speak the truth, uphold values and maintain the compassion and awareness needed to heal and serve. As a person practices

Kundalini Yoga, he can liberate and free himself from karma and discover and recognize his life's purpose or Dharma.

The practice of Kundalini Yoga, also called the "yoga of awareness," aims to awaken and arouse the dormant and sleeping Kundalini energy, which many believe is coiled at the base of the spine. The goal is to stir up the coiled energy to unravel and make its way up through the seven chakras that reside in the spine until it reaches and penetrates the seventh or crown chakra.

Performing and practicing exercises and breathing techniques, and meditation in Kundalini Yoga are essential in preparing the body, the mind, and the nervous system to handle the Kundalini energy as it awakens and begins ascending from the base of the spine to the crown chakra. Most of the physical exercises and postures focused mainly on the navel and spine area. Another main focus in this school of yoga are breathing techniques. Asanas or postures performed in Kundalini Yoga are done with specific pranayama or breathing techniques that aim to intensify the poses' effects. Poses and sequences are often performed rapidly and repetitively, together with a designated method of breathing. Other times, poses are held for certain periods while breathing in a specific manner. These practices free up the Kundalini energy that resides at the base of the spine, allowing it to travel upwards towards the head's crown eventually.

Before a person can bask in the light and splendor of the Kundalini energy, he must first go through a period of rigorous cleansing and purification and strength and conditioning the body and the nervous system. He must be the kind of person who possesses a firm and stable moral foundation. His values and beliefs must be solid and unyielding. He must have a certain degree of discipline that is not easily shaken and shattered. A person who seeks spiritual and Kundalini awakening must have only the purest intention of seeking and unraveling his true potential. He must walk in the path with an open heart and an open mind.

Kundalini Yoga is one of the safest ways to awaken the Kundalini. Through austere Yogic activities like pranayama, breath control, asanas or postures, meditation, and mantra chanting, a person's body, mind, and spirit are prepared to handle manage the arising Kundalini energy.

The process of spiritual and Kundalini awakening is something that you must approach with great care and respect. Although everyone has the Kundalini within, rousing it with the wrong intentions can only bring a person more harm than good. The act of awakening must stem from a pure heart. It must be a heart that seeks nothing but oneness with the Divine. A heart aspires and intends to use the powers that come with an awakened Kundalini for the greater good. It must be a heart that is open, compassionate, true, and kind. It must be a heart that seeks to heal and to serve.

Yoga for spiritual and Kundalini awakening must be employed and practiced in a loving manner of offering the self; the life forces and energies are released, liberated, and freed up in an easy, harmonious and safe way.

How to Increase the Potential of Your Body and Mind with the Kundalini Yoga

Being able to do it on your own is exactly what this book is about. However, if you want to do it with a spiritual master or guru's help, then this would involve complete dedication and submission to your master. Your master may also require you to do certain meditation practices; however, some claim to be able to awaken one's Kundalini as long as the disciple relinquishes everything and submits to his/her master. The problem here is that it is not easy to find a real master. Unfortunately, there are so many people out there who claim to be a master but are, in reality, just merely full of hacks and shams. Another problem with this approach is that although a master may be able to awaken your Kundalini, your soul might not be ready for it. This refers to your spiritual maturity. Therefore, when it comes to awakening the Kundalini, it is strongly advised that you do the work yourself so that your soul can mature and make you be ready for it. Of course, you are still free to ask help from a master but do not neglect your own spiritual growth.

It is probably safe to assume that your Kundalini lies dormant in the root of your spinal column right now, explaining why you are reading this book. Do not worry, as this book will guide you and teach you the techniques that will allow you to awaken the serpentine power. Just stay with me to gain knowledge as you follow me on this journey of true Kundalini awakening.

Releasing is a powerful practice that can help you awaken your Kundalini energy even more as it prevents you from constricting your energy and closing the space where Kundalini energy wants to flow.

Acceptance Equals Flow

As a part of our human conditioning, allowing things to simply happen without immediately jumping into a fear-based need to control everything can be challenging. We tend to like things done a certain way and frequently believe that if they don't happen the "right" way, that we are in some way doomed. Many individuals may even experience a sensation similar to that of a fear of death when things do not go according to plan.

You must understand that acceptance directly equals flow energy when it comes to life and life-force energy. Using flow energy to support your awakening will not only equate to a greater awakening experience, but it will also translate into less fear. Many people tend to attempt to resist due to fear, and in turn, they directly make their awakening painful. This is because they struggle to simply flow and instead feel as though they must control everything.

When you feel as though your awakening is painful, it is likely because you are resisting the flow of the energy. Imagine holding a bottle of soda and shaking it. The amount of pressure (energy) inside of the bottle would rapidly rise. Unless you removed the lid, it would have nowhere to go. As such, it would likely result in the bottle feeling very bloated and hard to the touch. Imagine this being yourself. When you choose to awaken Kundalini energy and then restrict the flow by refusing to accept things, you become overwhelmed with energy inside. The bloated and hard feeling that the soda bottle would have felt like would, for you, feel like pain and intense energy. You might feel like a volcano, even!

When you accept things as they are, it becomes a lot easier for you to release the need to be in control and allow things to happen naturally. Then, you can have a more positive experience with Kundalini energy, as opposed to feeling as though you are being ploughed down by intense energy buildup.

Releasing Fear

The first step to allowing things to flow is releasing fear. Fear is the energy that causes us to restrict. When we feel afraid of something, we may tense up, try to reduce the amount of space we take up, and even start shaking. Our bodies become much closed and our energy even more closed. If you live chronically in this state, or if you immediately turn into this state as a result of your awakening symptoms, you can end up feeling very overwhelmed by everything.

Releasing fear may seem challenging, but it is easier than you think. A great way to release fear is to simply lay in your bed at least once or twice a day and allow energy to move through you. Invite the energy to clear away anything that does not belong within you, and that is not serving you in your experience. This will help fear energy move out of you and a more positive form of awakened Kundalini energy flow through you.

Any time you feel fear arising, simply take a moment to invite your energies to clear themselves out. Take some time to notice what is going on within you. You may even use this as an opportunity to take some time to use a breathing meditation to help release any energy within you and relax more. Anything that allows you to release fear and choose love and acceptance will help immensely with your awakening process.

Releasing Daily Expectations

Many of us rise with expectations on how our day is going to play out. When our expectations are not met, or something does not go to plan, we end up feeling very upset and stressed out. This is an extreme form of stress that can easily be avoided by releasing daily expectations.

When you wake in the morning, take stock of what "needs" to happen. For example, perhaps you need to go to work or a doctor's appointment. Then, release expectations on everything else. Release expectations on how those activities will play out. Release expectations on what traffic will be like, whether or not you will remember to bring everything with you, and what will happen in between. Instead, allow yourself to hope for the best and do your best, but release expectations that everything will happen perfectly every time.

Releasing People that Bring You Pain

One of the parts of awakening that many people find quite challenging is releasing people from your life. You have likely been holding on to many people in your life that do not fit well. Many of the people we tend to keep in our lives when we are not operating from an awakened state tend to be toxic. Even though we may love them or feel obligated to keep them in our lives, this does not mean that they have a right to our relationship. You must remember that you do not owe anyone anything. If the person in question is someone you cannot avoid, say a coworker or a boss, and there is absolutely nothing you can do about it in the immediate moment, you need to minimize contact as much as possible.

Releasing Places that Bring You Pain

In addition to people that can bring you pain, you may also find that you have a tendency to continue frequenting places that bring you pain. These may not be obvious pains, but if they bring you discomfort or displeasure, you can guarantee that they bring some degree of suffering or pain.

The most common places people frequent that may bring pain into their lives include places like:

- Excessively busy grocery stores, or grocery stores that consistently sell poor quality foods
- Your place of work
- A family member or friend's house (often due to feelings of obligation)
- The mall, or other places to "hang out" that bring you discomfort
- A doctor or therapist's office where you do not feel supported by the doctor or therapist

There are many other places that you may be able to think of on your own as well. These places all share one thing in common: they bring discomfort or displeasure. Often, however, we tend to feel obligated to continue going to these places for one reason or another. While you may have to go to similar places, this does not mean you have to go to the exact locations that bring you discomfort or displeasure just because you have always done that. You can find a new grocery store that is enjoyable and that sells higher quality food. You can find a new place of work or hire a new doctor or therapist, rather than frequenting places that do not bring peace and contentment into your life. You do not have to hang out in places that keep you uncomfortable.

Ultimately, we tend to spend a lot of time in these places because human conditioning leads us to believe that we are supposed to do this. Then, we find ourselves frustrated and stressed out because these places do not please us. However, we rarely get into the root cause of the problem and find new practices! Take some time to consider any place in your life that causes any level of suffering, and eliminate those places or trade them out for places that bring joy and contentment into your life.

Releasing Old Cycles that Restrict Your Awakening

Humans are creatures of habit. Nearly everything we do is done in a circular motion or in cycles. Being aware of these cycles and eliminating them is a powerful way to remove ourselves from toxic cycles that are no longer serving our wellbeing. When we take a moment to address these cycles and choose differently, we empower ourselves to act differently.

This means we can begin taking on new cycles that are more aligned with our well-being.

Some common cycles we tend to experience but not recognize are those that become habitual. For example, say someone says something to you that triggers a bully from your childhood once said. So, you immediately begin feeling sad about yourself and who you are. Then, you begin feeling disempowered. You might turn to a comforting practice, such as eating, smoking, drinking, lying in bed, or virtually anything else as a means to try and comfort yourself from the pain. Then, after you comfort yourself, you resume your daily life. When the trigger is pulled again at a later date, you start the cycle all over again.

These cycles can consume us. As well, they rarely serve us in any way. In many cases, the cycles themselves are related to stuff that happened long ago. Sometimes, we have already healed from the trigger, but the cycle is so habitual that we continue to use it and never take the time to release it and replace it with a new cycle.

Anywhere that you notice habits like this taking place, take the time to consider why these habits exist and how you can go about reducing or eliminating them. Releasing unhealthy cycles that bring unnecessary suffering can have an extremely positive impact on your healing, as well as on supporting your Kundalini awakening.

Chapter 5: Physical, Mental and Sexual Benefits of Kundalini Yoga Practice

Clearing and Calming of the Mind

As with any practice which includes meditation, these practices will naturally clear your mind. When you allow yourself to meditate at least 15 minutes a day, you will see that even if you had a racing mind, it would start to calm down. This is a benefit that most people will find beneficial, even when starting with the Kundalini awakening process.

Improvement in Memory

With the combination of the pranayamas and yoga poses, you will be introducing more oxygen into your system. This, in turn, helps the blood to flow more easily throughout the body, including the brain. More blood entering the brain improves the cognitive functions and the pituitary and pineal glands.

Physical Ailments Can be Relieved or Cured

During the process of Kundalini awakening, you are working towards cleaning out your nadis and chakras to facilitate Kundalini Shakti's movement. This cleansing brings about an environment in your body that diseases cannot survive, so they will be greatly reduced or eradicated.

Increased Physical and Mental Strength

There is no doubt that the dutiful practice of yoga poses will get you into shape. Coupled with the other exercises in Kundalini, your mind will become sharper and focused, which in turn increases your mental fortitude. You will find that you will be able to control your emotions, as well.

Proven Build Up of Willpower

There is no doubt that some of these Kundalini exercises are difficult. There are some that you will need to practice other exercises before you even think about graduating yourself. With the need to continue to push yourself systematically strengthens your willpower and drives you to succeed.

Feeling One with the Universe

When you can connect with the higher energies within yourself, you will realize that we are all just from the same source. No matter what your background, education, upbringing, belief system, or marital status, we are based in the same energy of the Ultimate Consciousness.

Tap into Inner Intuition and Guides

As you dig deeper within yourself and can silence your thoughts, you will start to hear another voice that will never steer you wrong. This inner guide is your intuition, your gut feeling, which always has your higher interests at heart. Learn to trust this voice, and you will excel more quickly during the Kundalini awakening process.

Emotional Balance

Because you have strengthened your body and cleared your mind, body, and soul of troubling aspects which have occurred to you, this makes you more in control of your emotions, and you will find you simply will not react as much, if at all. You realize what the bigger picture is, and you do not allow petty things to ruin your day.

Feeling Overall Bliss and Peace

When you go through the Kundalini awakening process, there certainly are low points. However, just as quickly, you can be sent up to soaring heights which blow your mind. You cannot even imagine this state at this point in your journey. Feeling these emotions certainly makes up for any hardships you will go through.

Psychic Abilities Are Enhanced

You will find that you will become more sensitive to the sounds, colors, and vibrations around you. This happens when you come more in tune with your body and then it radiates from there. When your intuition becomes more enhanced, you will start to know everything that you need at the moment that you need it.

Slower Aging Process

When you get to the higher levels of Kundalini yoga practice, you will see a glow that will start to show in your skin. This is partly because of the cleaning process. It is also because you are balancing out the elements within your body to function more efficiently. Your body will no longer need to work so hard in maintaining itself.

Connection with the Divine

This is the ultimate goal of Kundalini yoga and awakening. When you can be in direct connection with the creator, anything is possible. You lose all earthly bounds and are able to achieve the so-called unachievable. Going back to the Source is the perfect prize for all of the hard work and dedication you have put into your practice.

Sacred Chant

Many of the chakras can be healed through a sacred chant. When you use a mantra, rhythm, and breath, it has been found to have beneficial effects on well-being and health. It can also bring joy to the heart and the soul. The sacred sound is known as Naad Yoga. The experience comes from how your voice's vibrations can have a positive effect on the body, the mind, and the spirit. In fact, the sound can change the chemicals in your brain.

Inner Soul Guidance

Through Kundalini Awakening and Kundalini Yoga, you will learn all about the power of your intuitive mind. As we mentioned before, you need to learn how to listen to the voice inside your head. Each person has this voice, but it is up to you to choose to listen to it. As you clear your mind, especially your subconscious mind, you will learn how to listen to your thoughts without needing to rely on others. This way, you can always be present and sense your intuition. The more you practice, the stronger your ability to face choices and decisions will come!

Karma

It is thought that it takes you out of the karma cycle when you practice Kundalini. As you begin to practice, your positive intention will grow, therefore putting you into Kundalini Kriyas. These are exercises that help you burn off karma. As you practice more, you will become more intuitive to your decisions as well as your conscious. As you do this, you will begin to walk on a Dharma path instead of living according to karma.

Spiritual Chain

As you now know, Kundalini has been taught for thousands of years. Originally, it was taught by the Master to the student. In a Kundalini Yoga class, you will chant, "Ong Namo Guru Dev Namo." As you do this, you will be linked to spiritual masters from the times before your existence. The lineage is known as The Golden Chain. Through spiritual awareness, it will guarantee Kundalini's teachings to make sure you will remain unadulterated and pure.

Emotional Balance

What you may not know is that by balancing your Kundalini, you will also be balancing your glands, purifying your blood, strengthening your nervous system, and cleaning out your subconscious. As you awaken your Kundalini, you will gain the strength to choose how you respond to your thoughts and feelings instead of just reacting. You will also have a greater awareness during your daily activities. As you practice more, you will also learn how to let your emotions go. No longer will you just react emotionally? By developing a neutral mind, you may find yourself living a more positive life. The key is to act instead of reacting.

No More Negativity

As you practice awakening your Kundalini, you will begin to expand your aura. This is the energy field that surrounds you. Its main job is to alert you of any positive or negative emotions around you. At this point, you probably have a weak aura. When it is weak, you can easily allow negative influences to affect you. As you strengthen your aura, it will keep you centered, and you will know your true identity.

New Lifestyle

In life, we make a lot of excuses that keep us unhappy. Luckily, Kundalini Yoga is meant for people with busy lives. That means that it can be done quickly and still work effectively. It is a yoga that can fit into many different lifestyles. Whether you attend weekly or bi-weekly, there are many benefits to be found. There are also yoga teachings that can change other parts of your life. Whether you want to change your hygiene, child-rearing, or conscious communication, there is yoga for that!

Relax

As we mentioned earlier, Kundalini yoga will work to strengthen your nervous system. If your nervous system is weak at this point, you are probably susceptible to stress. Through yoga, you will learn how to relax like you have never felt before. You may find that you will reach a rejuvenating state through yoga to bring you to total relaxation. Through regular practice, it can help you build resilience to stress and give you some extra stamina.

Community

On your journey, you do not need to do this alone. Often, yoga brings people together who are like-minded. This can be a very powerful tool as you travel along your consciousness journey. If you weren't already aware, many Kundalini yoga centers and studios could help welcome you into a community. With other people, you will develop a community that can meditate and chant together. It also helps to have people to help you make positive changes in your life.

Befriending Your Soul

As you practice Kundalini, you may begin to get a grip on your ego. You will slowly be learned about your soul's depth so you can learn the truth of your connection to your soul and the Universe. Through more practice, you will learn how to unite yourself with the Infinite. Gaining the experience can help you forget your insecurities of knowing who you are. This way, you will let go of the past and healthily manifest your destiny.

Chapter 6: What Are the Chakras

Chakras are the energy centers of the body. If the physical body has vital organs, then the spiritual or energy body has chakras. It is important to keep your chakras healthy, as unhealthy chakras would result in poor physical health. According to a study, before physical ailments manifest on the physical body, they first appear on the energy or spiritual body. The chakras are also points where energy can enter and leave the body. To awaken the Kundalini, you need to have strong and healthy chakras.

Since there is a link between the energy body and the physical body, you need to ensure that your chakras are clean and healthy. The chakras, especially the main chakras of the body, facilitate the free flow of energy.

When a person is sick, he is most likely to have some issues with one or more of his chakras.

It should be noted that the chakras do not just relate to your physical body, but they can also affect your life. For example, having a strong root chakra would mean that you have stability in life. If you have a healthy heart chakra, then the chances are that your life is full of harmony and love. As you can see, your chakras' status and health can have a significant influence on your life.

Psychic power can also be acquired by developing the chakras. Therefore, working on your chakras would be an important part of your training. Now, it should be noted that the body has seven main chakras. These seven chakras are found along the spine, starting from the base of the spine and up to the crown chakra, located a few inches above the head. Let us discuss them one by one.

The seven Chakras

The First Chakra— Root Chakras

The base chakra is the beginning of the energetic journey in the subtle body. Its Sanskrit name means "root." It is the Earth element. It is survival. It is the right "To Have." It is here that the Kundalini energy is stored. This is the place of physical health, grounded-ness, stability, youthful quality, vitality, fight or flight instinct, and prosperity.

This chakra is associated with the color red. It is located at the base of the spine and contains the energy there and surrounding the legs, feet, and gonads. It is connected to your sense of smell, the first sense you are aware of when you are born.

When your root chakra is balanced, you will feel secure, abundant, comfortable with yourself, centered, calm, grounded, and connected to nature and the earth.

When your root chakra is imbalanced, you may experience feelings of insecurity, anger, disconnection, depression, shortage of patience, nervousness, greed, unnecessary fear, and lack. When this imbalance manifests in our physical bodies, it may appear as frequent illness, obesity, eating disorders, constipation, knee troubles, sciatica, and even hemorrhoids.

Since the root chakra is where the dormant Kundalini energy lives and rises from when awakened, it is important to recognize the chakra's qualities and its connection to all the other chakras. However, one must not emphasize this energy and here is why: Kundalini awakening begins here, but it may also end in the root chakra. Some experiences show that it can be the last chakra to truly awaken. The rest of the transformation through the chakras may occur first but for true balance to be achieved, Kundalini's energy must return to the beginning to where the source of the energy awakening began.

The Second Chakra — Svadhisthana

The second chakra is also often called the sacral chakra. Its Sanskrit name means "sweetness." It is the element of Water. It is the place of emotion and sexuality. It is the right "To Feel." This is the place of pleasure, fluid movement, creativity, and passion.

This chakra is associated with the color orange and is located in the area just below the navel in your lower abdomen and is associated with the bladder, female reproductive organs, lymphatic system, and pelvis. It is connected to the sense of taste.

When your sacral chakra is balanced, you will feel happy, joyful, creative, passionate, and capable of connecting physically. This is also where the drive to procreate exists.

When your sacral chakra is imbalanced, you may feel unworthy, isolated, numb, stiff, overly sensitive, and emotional. You may also have a sexual addiction, or what is called sexual anorexia, hormone imbalance, and potential for miscarriages or difficulty conceiving.

This is a place where you block your emotions. Here is where you can restrict the flow of energy as a whole. It is important to do the emotional work necessary, recovering lost feelings and sometimes re-experiencing them so that you can heal and release them as you continue your awakening journey. Ultimately, when you heal and unblock your sacral chakra, you can allow a healthy flow of your emotional energy so you can experience pleasure through body movement and sexuality. Unblocking your sacral chakra can allow you to experience change, growth, and connection with your passionate self.

The Third Chakra — Manipura

The third chakra is also known as the solar plexus chakra. Its Sanskrit name means "lustrous gem." It is the element of Fire. It is power, and it is energy. It is the right "To Act." This is the place of personal power, the strength of will, and the sense of purpose.

This chakra is associated with the color yellow, and it is located between the area just below the navel and the base of the sternum. The physical feature associated with the solar chakra is the adrenal glands. Your adrenal glands regulate metabolism, blood pressure, and your immune system.

When the chakra is in balance, you will feel energy and drive, confidence, a sense of respect for others, as well as respect for the self, an active and cheerful disposition, and a strong sense of purpose.

An imbalance of the solar plexus chakra can represent as an arrogant demeanor, demanding attitude, overbearing sensibilities, and addictions. The opposite side of imbalance would look like a deficiency of energy, helplessness, a feeling of weakness, timidity, and a submissive life approach.

This chakra demonstrates a significant turning point in Kundalini awakening. It will cause a profound shift in your intentions, intuitions, self-value, and ability to see the beauty in the world. This is where judgment, biases, and prejudice melt away, first with the self and then the whole world around you. This is where you begin to feel your Kundalini power, but there is still so much more to go through.

The Fourth Chakra — Anahata

The fourth chakra is also known as the heart chakra. The Sanskrit name for this chakra translates to mean "unstuck," or unhurt, unbeaten. It is the element of Air. It is love and relationships. It is the right "To Love." This is the place of compassion for the self and others, acceptance of the self and others, and balance in all relationships.

When the heart chakra is in balance, you will feel love, compassion, interconnectedness, acceptance; life will flow smoothly. There will be a general feeling of affection for everyone and everything— Universal love.

If the heart chakra is imbalanced, it can express this through excessiveness or deficiency. A deficient heart chakra can often look like low self-worth or low self-esteem, melancholy, isolation, depression, inability to breathe deeply. Excessive heart chakra energy shows itself in the form of co-dependency, clingy behavior, and too much caretaking of others.

Interestingly, like with the extremes listed above, the heart chakra can spontaneously open for energetic flow from a newly experienced, deep love of someone. On the other end, extreme loss or grief can cause a shift and crack open.

Regardless of what causes the initial awakening of the heart chakra, be it the Kundalini awakening process, falling in love, or grieving a loss, it is sure to be an emotional roller-coaster. This can be aided with the Kundalini practices outlined in this book.

The Fifth Chakra — Vishuddhi

The fifth chakra is also called the throat chakra. The Sanskrit name for this chakra translated is "purification." It is the element of Ether or sound. It is communication. It is the right "To Speak." This is the place of self-expression, speaking, soul song, and the ability to communicate with others.

The color associated with this chakra is blue, and it is located at the throat. Several physical features are connected to this chakra, such as the already mentioned throat, jaw, neck, thyroid gland, teeth, ears, and esophagus; everything is associated with speaking and listening.

When this chakra is balanced, you can enjoy clear and truthful self-expression, honest and good communication, creative expression, and affinity with self and others. There is also an ability to comprehend the balance of opposite forces with reverence, accepting the value of both light and dark, high and low, and they each have a vital role in the harmony of all life energy.

When this chakra experiences imbalances or blockages, it can manifest as difficulty expressing oneself, inability to release wounds, pain or trauma because of suppressed emotions, sore throat, difficulty hearing, actual ear problems, tight neck and shoulders, and stagnant creative flow.

This chakra has a great deal to do with sound, so many methods for clearing blockages or opening and activating the throat chakra utilize singing or chanting, rhythm entrainment, and sound vibration.

The Sixth Chakra — Ajna

The sixth chakra is often called the brow chakra or third eye. The Sanskrit name for this chakra translates to mean "perceive" or to know. It is the element of Light. It is visual perception, intuition, clairvoyance. It is the right "To See." This is the place of imagination, thought, telepathy, vision, rational logic.

The sixth chakra is associated with the color indigo and is situated between the eyes or behind the eyebrows. Its physical attribute is the pituitary and pineal gland. The pituitary gland regulates hormone secretions, while the pineal gland regulates sleep patterns and circadian rhythms.

When the sixth chakra is balanced, there are great abilities in perception, your mind is at ease and can process thought quickly, improved memory and intelligence, lacking fear of death, you have a strong connection to your intuition. You can have clairvoyant and telepathic abilities surface.

An imbalance in the sixth chakra can manifest as headaches, mental health issues, and illnesses such as hallucinations and nightmares, paranoia, anxiety, and delusions. Because of its connection to sight and the eyes, it can also present itself as poor sight or visual perception.

Once this chakra becomes open and blockages begin to clear, energy can travel back down through the lower chakras for continued healing and cleansing, as there will likely be unresolved energy blocks still needing cleansing. That is why the Kundalini awakening process is an ongoing journey with the self.

The Seventh Chakra — Sahasrara

The seventh chakra is also often called the crown chakra. The Sanskrit name for this chakra translates to mean "thousand-fold." It is the element of thought. It is expanded consciousness. It is the right "To Know." This is the place of understanding, of enlightenment.

The crown chakra is associated with the color violet and is located at the top of the cerebral cortex's head. This chakra's physical component included the brain, hands, nervous system, and in part the pituitary gland, creating a link to the sixth chakra.

When the seventh chakra is balanced, you will have an expanded consciousness that will lead to a transcendence of barriers projected by humanity and the laws of nature, have a greater understanding and acceptance of death, mortality, and the immortality of the soul, increased and heightened spiritual gifts and capabilities, and the creation of miracles.

If your crown chakra is blocked, it can manifest as migraines, headaches, and general tension around the head. You may also feel alienated or isolated, suffer boredom, have an apathetic quality, disconnection, and lack comprehension or ability to learn and retain new information. It can also go in the direction of being a bit spacey, "in your head" all the time, and sometimes overly intellectual, preventing your ability to attain pure-consciousness.

The balancing or opening of this chakra in Kundalini awakening is closely connected to the third eye. The ability to transcend and experience enlightenment is the moving away from smaller patterns to welcome a deeper, broader perspective, one that encompasses all life and all matter, beyond the confines of limited thoughts and beliefs that keep our kundalini locked and dormant.

From the Root to the Head and Beyond

The system as a whole is a beautiful, throbbing and constantly vibrating energetic life force of its own. This chakra energy is always present and always fluctuating. When the Kundalini energy is activated at the base of your spine in your first chakra, you begin the upward journey that will cause you to face all the elements, qualities, blocks, deficiencies, and excesses of your chakras. It is the beginning of healing and awakening to your divine light and energy to become one with the power of creation. What you discover on this path, the path through the chakras will be how you come into contact with the true nature of yourself and all things.

Knowing about each chakra is important for the awakening process as it will give you the understanding to listen to your body. It is also important because they are the essential, energetic part of your being directly linked to Kundalini awakening experience. Take some time to listen to each part of your body, each chakra system, and develop a relationship to each energy so that you can be connected to the whole of your subtle body.

How to Clear and Balance the Chakras

Try allowing one week of focus for each chakra and listen along the way to whether or not you need to offer more, or less time, to each energy. Your body is always talking to you. Listen to it.

Root Chakra: Muladhara

Your root chakra is connected to the element Earth. One great way to help clear the energy in your root is to be in nature. Think about tree roots. Where do tree roots want to be? In the forest, in the soil, near the rivers and streams, in the mountains. Healing your root chakra involves a connection to nature. Take off your shoes and walk along the beach. Find a secluded nature trail and spend time reaching out and touching plant life, trees, moss, and soil. Go on a camping trip and live in the woods for a couple of days. While you are there, collect some nature treasures like stones, feathers, driftwood, and mosses to take home. Find a space in your home and create a nature altar.

If you can't make it out to the woods or live in a city without a lot of nature access, go to your local nursery or garden center and walk around in it. Get a few potted houseplants to take home and make a part of your world. Find out what the plants need and want and tend to them.

Your root chakra is also the color red. You can do a lot of energy clearing by working with and using the color red. Grow or gather red flowers to decorate your home. Dress your body in color red with a red outfit, scarf, or other accents. Construct an altar to the color red using red candles, ornaments, or artwork you like, and light the candles every day to honor your root chakra.

In addition to wearing red, or decorating with it, you can also eat it! While working with your root chakra energy and balancing it, consume red-colored foods and tea. Red meat and proteins are associated with the chakra, but if you don't eat meat, that's okay! There are plenty of other red-colored foods like beets, apples, raspberries, tomatoes, red bell peppers, and more.

Another way to focus on your root chakra energy is to use healing stones and crystals. Each chakra usually has a collection of stones and crystals ideal for energy clearing in that area. Some of those for the root chakra are red jasper, red carnelian, bloodstone, black tourmaline, obsidian, smoky quartz, red garnet, hematite, and more. Not all of these stones are red, and they don't need to be. They have grounding qualities that are ideal for working with your root chakra.

You can also intonate the sound associated with this chakra which is "I am." Sit in front of your earth altar or red-colored altar (or both!) and take some time to use long inhales and exhales to intone "I am." Focus on the color red in the base of your spine, its brightness throbbing and releasing negativity.

As you work with this chakra and become more connected to it, trust your intuition to guide you. You may come up with several other ways not listed here to cleanse your root. Listen to your higher mind and let it guide you.

Sacral Chakra: Svadhisthana

The sacral chakra is connected to the water element, and when you are working with devotion to healing this chakra, you will need to bring water energy into your world. If you have access to a swimming pool or hot tub, that would be a great way to be in the water. (Note of caution: many swimming pools and hot tubs have high amounts of chlorine which is damaging and will feel disruptive to your energy clearing). If you prefer another method of being in the water, swimming in a lake, or even taking off your socks and shoes and putting them in a flowing stream, or river would be a great approach, or just sit in the rain! You can also take long baths, submerging your whole head underwater periodically to cover your whole body in the water element.

The sacral chakra is the color orange and should be worked with when clearing energy here. Dress in this color, or accent your clothes with this color. You can also plant orange flowers in your garden or keep cut orange flowers in your home. Orange foods should be consumed, and the fun part is discovering how many foods and liquids are orange. Remember to stay away from processed foods and artificial sweeteners. They just create more disharmony and blocked energy. Some examples of orange foods are carrots, oranges, mango, melons, orange bell peppers, sweet potatoes, and tangerines. Have fun finding more of them!

Healing stones and crystals for this chakra are not always orange, but many of them tend to be. Some of them are orange calcite, citrine, orange carnelian, orange aventurine, orange kyanite, and tiger's eye. You can lay on the floor and place one or more of these stones in the area of your sacral chakra, on your lower abdomen, while you breathe and meditate on the color orange, filling you with bright light and clearing away any blocks or negativity.

Create an altar to your sacral chakra with orange candles, flowers, and images that speak to this energy's qualities. Place a bowl of water on the altar and keep it clean and clear. If you like, put some of your orange crystals in the water bowl to charge the water and drink it at the end of a meditation.

The sound to use regarding this chakra is "vam." Sit in front of your altar and with candles lit and intone "vam" while you meditate on clearing this energy.

Allow any feelings and emotions to rise to be felt. This is the seat of emotion, and many things that have been bottled-up and repressed can come up when working with this energy. Keep a journal of your feelings as you spend time with this chakra, and trust your instinct to stay with this chakra until you are ready to move on to the next.

Solar Plexus Chakra: Manipura

In the third chakra, you find the element of Fire. Fire is a wonderful way you can clear energy. If you have a fireplace in your home that you rarely use, or only in the wintertime, make use of it for the ritual of heat and the power of light. You can also make a fire pit in your yard and have an outdoor bonfire. If neither of these is an option for you, you can always just use candlelight to bring fire close to you or into your home for the energy clearing benefits it will have to your solar plexus. Be sure to practice good fire safety with these kinds of rituals.

Since this is the place of personal power, drive, and a sense of purpose, you can use fire to bring attention to these aspects of yourself. Do you lack confidence? Are you feeling a lack of esteem for your purpose in life? Write down on a piece of paper any negative feelings you may have around your self-worth. Write that you desire to release that energy from your body. Reread it yourself out loud, and then fold it up as small as you like. Find a safe place, either outside, in a fireplace, or in an area or container in your home that will safely contain the fire. Set the paper on fire and watch it burn until it has gone to ashes. Then, take a new piece of paper and write down positive words about your strength, power, and purpose. Use statements like:

- I am comfortable in my power.
- I manifest the things I desire in my life easier.
- I let go of self-judgment and judgment of others.
- I am worthy.
- I do not need to be in control of everything.
- I am confident in who I am.

Once you have filled the page with these positive affirmations, read them aloud to yourself. Do it more than once if you need the message to sink in. Then, as you did with the first page, find a safe place to burn the paper. As you watch it burn away, let the golden flame infuse the message into you. Fully receive the message of your words as the fire brings it into reality.

If you feel concerned about using fire, just use the sun as your source of flame. Sunbathe, but don't get burned. The best time of day to enjoy sunbathing's healthful benefits is before 11 AM and a few hours before sunset, depending on the time of year.

Another component to work with is the color yellow. Yellow is the solar plexus chakra and is associated with the sun. Dress your body in yellow, or accent your clothes with the color. Bring yellow flowers into the home and build your Third Chakra altar with yellow candles and adornments.

Some of the healing stones and crystals for this chakra are golden amber, citrine, lemon quartz, golden tiger's eye, yellow tourmaline, and yellow jasper. Keep them on your altar, or wear them on your person. You can also clear any negative energy they might absorb by setting them in the sun to recharge and clear them.

There are plenty of yellow foods and teas you can eat as well! Bananas, pineapple, some melons, corn and grains, yellow bell peppers, and more. You can also make rejuvenating teas or tonics with ginger, turmeric, and chamomile and add a lemon to it for an extra dash of yellow.

Be sure to move your body as often as feel comfortable when working with this chakra. It is the seat of vitality and puts a spring in your step when open and balanced. Do some dancing or power walking. If you sit at a desk a lot, set a timer to get up and move around every 30 minutes.

Feel your power as you work with this chakra. Use the sound associated with this energy, "ram" to really tune into this power. Intone "ram" while you stand in the sunlight or in front of your bonfire. Do not be afraid of how powerful you are. You are so powerful and you deserve to shine like the yellow sun!

Heart Chakra: Anahata

The heart chakra brings the element of air. Air is all around us. You breathe it in and let some out. It changes the weather and cleanses out old, stagnant energy with one gust. Work with this energy and help clear and balance the heart chakra and find ways to get closer to this element. When you drive your car, turn off the air conditioner and drive with the wind in your hair. When you sleep at night, crack some windows and allow the fresh morning air to gently blow in while you wake up for a new day. If you are comfortable and can go even further, take a boat ride to feel some fresh air on your face as you coast around the water, or try paragliding to put some wind in your sails. At the very least, adopt a daily practice, morning and night, of healthful breathing exercises. They can be a part of your morning meditations or evening yoga practice. You can also just breathe. Take some time throughout the day to stop whatever you are doing and mindfully focus on your breath.

Eat green! Tons of foods are green, and not only is it good to focus on this food color while you are healing your heart, but it's also just great to eat a lot of vegetables, which so many green foods are. Some ideas for green foods to add to your heart chakra healing are broccoli, avocado, kiwi, kale, leafy greens, Brussels sprouts, spinach, herbs like rosemary, basil, and thyme, green apples, bok choy, and so much more. Do your best to steer clear of processed foods, artificial colors, and sweeteners, alcohol, and a lot of caffeine.

Make your heart altar in the color green. Use green candles and anything you like that has this color. You can collect things from nature that are green or use green stones and crystals. Some of these for the heart chakra are green calcite, rose quartz, malachite, jade, rhodonite, and green aventurine. You can also wear these on your person as their energy will help remove blockages and create balance. Wear them with your green outfits or accent colors.

Bringing more of the color green into your life can also involve adding some new, luscious potted plants into your house. When you build your altar, put it with all of your houseplants so you have all the greenery in one place while you devote your attention to your heart chakra.

Sit among all the green and place your hand over your heart. Breathe in and out several times, deeply. Breath in loving thoughts and energy, breathe out negativity held in the heart. Say aloud or in the mind-heart healing affirmations such as:

- I love myself unconditionally.
- I forgive myself fully.
- I am open to giving and receiving love.
- I deserve to love and be loved.
- I am worthy of healthy and loving relationships.

You can say this every day, or multiple times a day to really help your energy clear here. So many of us have large blocks in our heart chakra. An open heart is so important to fully awaken your Kundalini power.

For even more opening, intone the heart chakra sound, "yum." Put your hands over your heart as you intone this sound and feel the vibration of "yum" in your chest.

Throat Chakra: Vishuddhi

As you rise further up in the chakras, you rise further up in the elements. You started with the roots in the earthy soil, through the rivers and streams to the hot hearth and into the airy wind, and now, in the fifth chakra, you come to the element of Ether. This is where the clouds are. Your throat chakra is connected to this element and when working with this etheric energy finds ways to get closer to the heavens. By simply laying outside and doing some good, old-fashioned cloud gazing, you can connect with the vibration of ether. Forget about your body for a moment and watch the clouds drift by. Another option, if you are feeling particularly bold from opening up your solar plexus, you can take a hot air balloon ride or try skydiving. That's about the closest you can get to the clouds if you are not an airline pilot.

Wearing blue, as with the other chakras, while you focus on this energy, will be of great benefit. You can use blue accents in your house. Blue flowers are harder to come by unless dyed, but hydrangea, which incidentally looks like a puffy cloud, would be a perfect choice for your home or altar. Some of the stones that will be useful for clearing energy in the throat are azurite, turquoise, lapis lazuli, labradorite, sodalite, and moonstone. Wear them on your body, or, as with any other of the chakras, you can lay down on the floor and place one of these stones on your throat chakra and meditate on blue light infusing the energy of this chakra, clearing away any blocks or negativity.

Eat blue foods! Again, like with flowers, there isn't a surplus of blue-colored foods, but there are certainly enough to bring into your diet for the nutrition of this chakra. Some blue foods are blueberries, Adirondack blue potatoes, some seaweeds such as kelp, microalgae, indigo milk cap mushrooms, and blue corn. Also, fruit, in general, is the preferred food of the throat chakra. Borage is an excellent, blue-colored flower to use as an herbal tea that provides antioxidants, minerals and vitamin C. Mostly just the stem and leaf is used for the tea, but the star-shaped flowers would like stunning on your altar.

Sing! The throat chakra is your true voice. Bringing your words and sounds up through your throat while working with this energy is vitally important. Sing your favorite songs in your car, in the shower. If you don't feel ready to sing, you can whistle, or hum and let the song come later. Another way to exercise your throat chakra power is to write. Even if you are not speaking them, writing words are still using your voice. Keep a journal separate from your other chakra work just for your throat chakra. You may have more to say than you realize and may need extra space. Try not to overthink the writing, either. It is just for you, so let it flow out of you. You can even just close your eyes and let the pen take over. Don't worry if it's legible, just write!

Finally, the sound to use with this chakra is "ham." Even if you haven't used this technique with the other chakras, since this chakra is about your true voice, it would be valuable to use the practice of intoning "ham" while you work with this energy. As you clear any blocks in this chakra, let go of any control you may have over your voice, speech, or what words want to come out. Let it flow. You can even record your voice speaking, singing, or intoning. Get connected to your voice and let it sing!

Brow Chakra: Ajna

Here, in the third eye, or brow chakra, we come to the element of light. You have made it through the ether and have now entered the space of starlight and the sun. Without light, we would not exist, for the Earth would be too cold to support life. The light of the sun brings the light of day, and the light of stars brings us light at night to show us the way. There are so many ways to work with the element of light while focusing on clearing your brow chakra. Clearing the way for light to shine here is so important to your arising Kundalini energy because it is here that you will get to see beyond all the earthly elements and into enlightenment. The word enlightenment has the word "light" in it. To bring light to the dark is part of Kundalini awakening.

Ways to enjoy light in this chakra devotion would be enjoying the sunshine, stargazing in a place where you can get a really good view of them, moon-gazing as it becomes full, and celebrating with moonlight rituals, hanging strings of lights in your garden, or inside your home to add some extra glow, candles on the altar or all around the home and seeing a light show. If you plan to visit or live near the Aurora Borealis light, that would be an excellent way to heal the third eye.

The third eye is connected to the color indigo. Like with all the other chakras, creating your altar with indigo colors, adornments, colors, plants, and flowers would be an excellent way to work with this energy and wear the color or accessorizing with it. Healing crystals and stones you can wear or use in meditations are amethyst, purple fluorite, iolite, indigo kyanite, moldavite, and black obsidian, to name a few. You can place one of these stones on your third eye as you lie on the floor in meditations. While opening and cleansing this energy, you may feel tingling, twinges, or tightness in this area, and it is perfectly normal.

Indigo and purple foods to enjoy during your third eye opening are purple kale, blackberries, grapes, and natural juices of this color, purple cabbage, figs, and much more.

The sound connected to the third eye is "sham." You can intone this sound while you do your meditations and while balancing one of your healing crystals on your brow as you lie on the floor.

The third eye is about your intuition, and exercising that power will be part of working with this energy. A lot of that is trusting the impulses, senses, or visions you may get during this phase of opening. Allow your imagination to flow. Keep a journal of your dreams and visions. You may begin to notice repetitive signs or symbols and numbers popping up a lot. Study their meaning to help you gain universal knowledge. It is also important to just listen and practice silence. You can hear and see into your third eye so much better when you cultivate time in your life for quiet. Listen to your wisdom, and it is already within you.

Crown Chakra: Sahasrara

Now, we have arrived at the crown, the seventh chakra, and the final point of the journey. Remember that you may repeat spontaneous and guided energy clearing in all of these chakras through Kundalini awakening. Sometimes, the energy must continue the journey back down through the earthly chakras before true awakening can occur. These practices are your opening to ascension and can be practiced regularly along the journey.

The crown chakra is ALL the elements connected in unity and oneness. This is the chakra where you can bring all the colors, all the sounds, and all the elements together in equal support of each other. It is associated with the color violet. Make this color the central color of your altar, clothing, and practice. You can include all the other colors as accents to the color violet. Put your altar together so that you honor the crown and place all the other chakra candles and adornments around this central color. This will also create a way for you to look back on the process of what you have already accomplished in your meditations, reflections, and energy, clearing focus with each chakra. You will see with your own eyes how they are all connected in the end.

The seventh chakra does not require nourishment with food or earthly sustenance. This would be a good part of the journey to try a juice cleanse or healthy, safe food-fasting period.

Energy cleansing and balancing stones and crystals for the crown chakra are selenite, clear quartz, okenite, charoite, eudialyte, and amethyst, to name a few. Sit in meditation in front of your altar with one of these balanced on the top of your head. Work your energy from your root through all the chakras to the crown of your head. Imagine this energy rising inside of you as a bright violet light. Let any images, sensations, thoughts, or feelings come to you and practice curiosity with each one. Do not try to identify or overthink any of this. Just curiously see, or listen as you vibrate with violet light energy. Breathe slowly and deeply—practice self-reflection without judgment, negativity, or classification. Just sit and "see" in your mind. Keep a notebook nearby because you may want to record any experiences to look at later.

By the time you reach the crown chakra and have explored the other chakras, working with healing, cleansing and balancing, you will be in a position to mentally, physically, and spiritually feel and understand your true self. Here you will sense and understand the truth of your connection to the whole universe and all the beings and energies contained in it. This is where you start to feel your spiritual connection truly and can see the path to enlightenment. Spend time knowing this. Spend time listening to it in your "eye." Give yourself permission and the freedom to just BE. Spend time in connection to the rhythmic vibration of the cosmos. Let go of the concept of time and listen to your divine power. It is awakened inside of you.

How to Awaken the Chakra

The human body contains three channels through which energy flows. The Ida Nadi, the left channel, corresponds with the moon and the sense of darkness that the moon brings to earth. The left channel corresponds to your desires and emotions and the events of your past. When its energy is pure and clean, it represents the qualities of art, music, compassion, love, and deep joy. If your left channel is blocked, you may experience feelings of guilt, low self-esteem, depression, and problems with your emotional attachments. The Pingala Nadi, the right track, corresponds to the sun and the light and heat it brings to the earth. The right channel controls your planning and actions. When the right channel is open, you will feel emotionally healthy and stable. When it is blocked, you will feel hatred, anger, pride, arrogance, and self-centered behavior like selfishness. The central channel creates a balance between the left and the right track. The central channel allows the Kundalini to ascend through the chakras toward the Crown Chakra. This chakra is where the power that guides you consciously and unconsciously flows through. It brings you to your higher self-awareness.

When you consciously switch your attention to your central channel during your efforts to awaken your Kundalini, your self-awareness will begin to evolve, and your attention will stop wildly swinging between current and past events. The left and right sides will start to lose their influence, and your attention will remain centered on your awakening efforts. You will experience real joy and inner peace by learning to exist in the present.

Your Kundalini energy has been present in your body since you were born, and it will remain with you until you die. It lies dormant in most people unless it is intentionally awakened in the pursuit of higher self-awareness. Your level of consciousness depends on the direction that your energy flows in the central channel. When your physical and emotional energy is lagging, that is a sign that your Kundalini energy is now flowing upward as it needs to flow. The Crown Chakra and the chakra just below it, the Third Eye Chakra, are spiritual magnets that pull the power of the Kundalini upward to facilitate a union with your higher self. Your ego is a magnet at the base of your spine that tries to pull the energy back toward it, taking you back into unawareness, selfishness, and negativity. The ego will draw your mind away from peaceful meditation by interrupting the flow of mindlessness.

The energy of the Kundalini lies coiled and asleep at the base of your spine. As it begins to awaken, it will rise through the central channel, past the lower six chakras, and into the Crown Chakra, where it will lead you into your higher consciousness and your real purpose. The awakening energy will energize the lower six internal chakras to make way for the Kundalini to arise and travel upward. Your inner chakras are small circuits of energy that lie all along your spine. As your Kundalini awakens, you will gain new knowledge of your life and its experiences. The clarity that comes from this energy will enable more power to flow freely through your body. As the energy moves upward through the central channel, it will pass the chakras until it encounters a blockage, and then the power will work to remove the blockage so it can continue its upward travel. The Kundalini is intelligent energy, and it will do what is needed to open the chakras so it can attain its goal of spiritual awakening.

Chapter 7: Meditation for the Seven Chakras

Chakra Meditations

Meditation gives you the power to transform your mind. It is meant to positively change your emotions, improve your concentration, and bring you a sense of calm. Through different meditation practices, you can train your mind to new patterns. With chakra meditations, you will be focusing your mind on your chakras to help clear them of blocked energies.

Root Chakra Meditation

This mediation is a tried-and-true method of creating a connection with your root chakra.

Find a comfortable position, either laying down or sitting, and take in three deep and slow breaths. Imagine the breath sending energy to your perineum; this is the space between your anus and genitals. With every exhale, release whatever you are holding in this area. This could be pain or fear. It could even be what you think you should feel while in this meditation.

Begin to gently tap at the top of your pubic bone or on either side of your hips' lower parts. This will wake up the connection you have with your root chakra.

As you continue to breathe in and out through your nose, direct your breath to your chakra. Picture a red glowing light growing and pulsing in your lower pubic area. For people who identify mostly as male, the light should spin clockwise. For people who identify mostly as female, the light should spin counterclockwise.

As you fall further into your meditative state, talk to your root chakra to see what it needs. Take some more breaths to notice if you get any feedback. This feedback could be a word, intuition, color, image, song, sound, or feeling. Act upon the feedback you receive. If nothing comes up, you don't need to worry about it. You will get something as you continue to practice.

If you didn't receive a message but you start to feel a new awareness in your root chakra, something like a pulsating in the lower hips and down through your feet, you have made a connection to your root chakra.

As your meditation comes to a close, take three deep and slow breaths. Direct your inhales towards your feet so that you are grounded, and then slowly open your eyes.

Make sure you take things slowly as you start. This will take some time and practice so be patient. If you end up feeling any sort of pain in your legs or lower back, you are trying too hard. Take a break and go back to it later. Remember that even seasoned meditators will sometimes find it hard to shut off their mind. Take this moment to observe these thoughts without judging them; let them go and gently refocus your mind.

Sacral Chakra Meditation

Find a comfortable position, either laying down or sitting. Take in three deep and slow breaths. With each inhale, imagine the breath sending energy to space right below your belly button. With every exhale, release whatever you are holding in this area. This could be pain or fear. It could even be what you think you should feel while in this meditation. You can place your hand on this area while you meditate if you would like.

Begin to tap the area below your bellybutton with two fingers gently. You can also gently massage the area in a circular motion.

As you continue to breathe in and out through your nose, direct your breath to your chakra. Picture an orange glowing light growing and pulsing in your lower abdomen area. For people who identify mostly as male, the light should spin clockwise. For people who identify mostly as female, the light should spin counterclockwise.

As you fall further into your meditative state, talk to your sacral chakra to see what it needs. Take some more breaths to notice if you get any feedback. This feedback could be a word, intuition, color, image, song, sound, or feeling. Act upon the feedback you receive. If nothing comes up, you don't need to worry about it. You will get something as you continue to practice.

If you didn't receive a message, but you start to feel a new awareness in your sacral chakra, something like a pulsating in this area, you have made a connection to your sacral chakra.

As your meditation comes to a close, take three deep and slow breaths. Direct your inhales towards your feet so that you are grounded, and then slowly open your eyes.

Make sure you take things slowly as you start. This will take some time and practice, so be patient. If you end up feeling any sort of pain in your lower abdomen, you are trying too hard. Take a break and go back to it later.

Solar Plexus Chakra Meditations

Find a comfortable position, either laying down or sitting. Take in three deep and slow breaths. With each inhale, imagine the breath sending energy to space right above your belly button. With every exhale, release whatever you are holding in this area. This could be pain or fear. It could even be what you think you should feel while in this meditation. You can place your hand on this area while you meditate if you would like.

Begin to gently tap the area above your belly button with two fingers. You can also gently massage the area in a circular motion.

As you continue to breathe in and out through your nose, direct your breath to your chakra. Picture a yellow glowing light growing and pulsing in your upper abdomen area. For people who identify mostly as male, the light should spin clockwise. For people who identify mostly as female, the light should spin counterclockwise.

As you fall further into your meditative state, talk to your solar plexus chakra to see what it needs. Take some more breaths to notice if you get any feedback. This feedback could be a word, intuition, color, image, song, sound, or feeling. Act upon the feedback you receive. If nothing comes up, you don't need to worry about it. You will get something as you continue to practice.

If you didn't receive a message, but you start to feel a new awareness in your solar plexus chakra, something like a pulsating in this area, you have made a connection to your solar plexus chakra.

As your meditation comes to a close, take three deep and slow breaths. Direct your inhales towards your feet so that you are grounded, and then slowly open your eyes.

Make sure you take things slowly as you start. This will take some time and practice so be patient. If you end up feeling any sort of pain in your upper abdomen, you are trying too hard. Take a break and go back to it later.

Heart Chakra Meditation

Find a comfortable position, either laying down or sitting. Take in three deep and slow breaths. With each inhale, imagine the breath sending energy to the center of your chest. With every exhale, release whatever you are holding in this area. This could be pain or fear. It could even be what you think you should feel while in this meditation. You can place your hand on this area while you meditate if you would like.

Begin to tap your chest with two fingers gently. You can also gently massage the area in a circular motion.

As you continue to breathe in and out through your nose, direct your breath to your chakra. Picture a glowing green light growing and pulsing in your chest. For people who identify mostly as male, the light should spin clockwise. For people who identify mostly as female, the light should spin counterclockwise.

As you fall further into your meditative state, talk to your heart chakra to see what it needs. Take some more breaths to notice if you get any feedback. This feedback could be a word, intuition, color, image, song, sound, or feeling. Act upon the feedback you receive. If nothing comes up, you don't need to worry about it. You will get something as you continue to practice.

If you didn't receive a message but you start to feel a new awareness in your heart chakra, something like a pulsating in this area, you have made a connection to your heart chakra.

As your meditation comes to a close, take three deep and slow breaths. Direct your inhales towards your feet so that you are grounded, and then slowly open your eyes.

Make sure you take things slowly as you start. This will take some time and practice so be patient. If you end up noticing your heart is racing uncomfortably, you are trying too hard. Take a break and go back to it later.

Throat Chakra Meditation

Find a comfortable position, either laying down or sitting. Take in three deep and slow breaths. With each inhale, imagine the breath sending energy to the notch of your throat. With every exhale, release whatever you are holding in this area. This could be pain or fear. It could even be what you think you should feel while in this meditation.

Begin to gently tap the bone at the notch of your throat with two fingers. You can also gently massage the area in a circular motion.

As you continue to breathe in and out through your nose, direct your breath to your chakra. Picture a glowing blue light growing and pulsing in your throat. For people who identify mostly as male, the light should spin clockwise. For people who identify mostly as female, the light should spin counterclockwise.

As you fall further into your meditative state, talk to your throat chakra to see what it needs. Take some more breaths to notice if you get any feedback. This feedback could be a word, intuition, color, image, song, sound, or feeling. Act upon the feedback you receive. If nothing comes up, you don't need to worry about it. You will get something as you continue to practice.

If you didn't receive a message, but you start to feel a new awareness in your throat chakra, something like a pulsating in this area, you have made a connection to your throat chakra.

As your meditation comes to a close, take three deep and slow breaths. Direct your inhales towards your feet so that you are grounded, and then slowly open your eyes.

Make sure you take things slowly as you start. This will take some time and practice so be patient. If you end up feeling any sort of pain in your neck, you are trying too hard. Take a break and go back to it later.

Third Eye Chakra Meditation

Find a comfortable position, either laying down or sitting. Take in three deep and slow breaths. With each inhale, imagine the breath sending energy to space between your brows. With every exhale, release whatever you are holding in this area. This could be pain or fear. It could even be what you think you should feel while in this meditation.

Begin to tap the area between your eyebrows with two fingers gently. You can also gently massage the area in a circular motion.

As you continue to breathe in and out through your nose, direct your breath to your chakra. Picture a glowing indigo light growing and pulsing in the area between your brows. For people who identify mostly as male, the light should spin clockwise. For people who identify mostly as female, the light should spin counterclockwise.

As you fall further into your meditative state, talk to your third eye chakra to see what it needs. Take some more breaths to notice if you get any feedback. This feedback could be a word, intuition, color, image, song, sound, or feeling. Act upon the feedback you receive. If nothing comes up, you don't need to worry about it. You will get something as you continue to practice.

If you didn't receive a message, but you start to feel a new awareness in your third eye chakra, something like a pulsating in this area, you have made a connection to your third eye chakra.

As your meditation comes to a close, take three deep and slow breaths. Direct your inhales towards your feet so that you are grounded, and then slowly open your eyes.

Make sure you take things slowly as you start. This will take some time and practice so be patient. If you feel like you are getting a headache at the front of your head, you are trying too hard. Take a break and go back to it later.

Crown Chakra Meditation

Find a comfortable position, either laying down or sitting. Take in three deep and slow breaths. With each inhale, imagine the breath sending energy to the top of your head. With every exhale, release whatever you are holding in this area. This could be pain or fear. It could even be what you think you should feel while in this meditation.

Begin to tap the top of your head two fingers gently. You can also gently massage the area in a circular motion.

As you continue to breathe in and out through your nose, direct your breath to your chakra. Picture a purple glowing light growing and pulsing in the top of your head. For people who identify mostly as male, the light should spin clockwise. For people who identify mostly as female, the light should spin counterclockwise.

As you fall further into your meditative state, talk to your crown chakra to see what it needs. Take some more breaths to notice if you get any feedback. This feedback could be a word, intuition, color, image, song, sound, or feeling. Act upon the feedback you receive. If nothing comes up, you don't need to worry about it. You will get something as you continue to practice.

If you didn't receive a message but you start to feel a new awareness in your crown chakra, something like a pulsating in this area, you have made a connection to your crown chakra.

As your meditation comes to a close, take three deep and slow breaths. Direct your inhales towards your feet so that you are grounded, and then slowly open your eyes.

Make sure you take things slowly as you start. This will take some time and practice so be patient. If you end up feeling any sort of pain in your head, you are trying too hard. Take a break and go back to it later.

Multiple Chakra Meditation

Begin by lying down. While relaxing, try to direct a slow inhale towards your root chakra and slowly exhale the energy through your mouth. Take three more breaths, and release anything that is stored in your root chakra. Get in touch with emotions that you may find in this chakra. You might even find a little bit of discomfort. Notice whatever is going on here. Picture a red ball of light healing your chakra. See if the initial sensations have changed.

Move up to your sacral chakra. Again, breathe into the chakra, and release whatever is being held there. Notice any sensations or feelings. Visualize an orange ball of light healing your sacral chakra. Take note of any changes that happen in this chakra.

Turn your focus to the solar plexus chakra. Breathe into this chakra, noticing any sort of emotion or sensations. Picture a large yellow ball of light healing this chakra. Notice if you feel any changes.

Moving up to your heart chakra, breathe into the chakra. Take note of any sensations or emotions that live here. Imagine a large green ball of light healing this chakra. See if any changes happen.

Focus on your throat chakra now. Breathe healing energy into it, and release anything that is there. Notice any sensations or feelings. Imagine a large blue light healing this chakra. Notice if any changes happen.

Slide up to your third eye chakra. Breathe into the chakra, and notice any sensations or emotions that are here. Imagine a large indigo light healing this chakra. Take note of changes that happen.

Move up to your crown chakra. Breathe into your chakra, and take note of any emotions or sensations that you are experiencing here. Picture a large purple light healing this chakra. Notice any changes that happen.

Take a moment to feel all of your chakras working together. Imagine a white light enveloping your body and healing your chakras. Lie here for a few more minutes allowing the white light to heal your body. Once you feel you have meditated long enough, take three deep breaths and slowly open your eyes.

Violet Flame

With this meditation, you can access fifth-dimensional frequencies that will help you to get rid of any unresolved and unhealed energies. This is an important thing to do when you want to clear out your chakras. Your chakras can't heal until you can heal from things that have happened to you. Things, good and bad, tend to hang around in our energy field. Until you can change the negative into light and love, you will suffer from chaos and negativity. Violet flame can help you to change this. When you enter the fifth dimension, you will be connected to those you love, no matter where they are. You will also see that everybody is connected energetically as one. When you are here, your life will unfold through your passion because you will naturally choose what brings you joy.

Find a quiet space where you won't be disturbed and get into a comfortable position. Sit so that your spine is straight and your arms and legs are uncrossed. Your feet should be flat on the floor with your hands rested in your lap.

As you breathe in, imagine you are breathing in white light or love through your heart chakra. Stay with this for a moment until you can feel it. This works the best when you feel you are devoted to forgiveness and love. If you are finding this hard to do, try to think of a person who was kind to you. Find a memory of them and relax into their kind and warm energy.

Take some time with this. Once you start to feel an opening, breathe the kindness out to somebody else. This will allow your heart chakra to open.

To start your meditation, begin with a decree like, "I am calling the violet flame to purify all that is inside of me." You can make your statement whatever you want as long as it starts with the words "I AM". Repeat this statement a few times out loud, and notice your thoughts and feelings. It will work more powerfully if you can speak it out loud instead of saying it in your head. You need to stay in a forgiving and loving mindset. You can continue to repeat this phrase as often as you want.

Once you feel you are centered, you can begin to speak your violet flame meditation. This is very different than other meditation because you speak through it. You can change this up however you would like.

"I am me. I am a presence. I breathe love into my heart. I am the center of the light. I call the complete power of the violet flame to change the memories, records, habits, effects, core, and causes of all of my actions, words, feelings, and thoughts I have ever used at any moment or in any dimension, unknown or known that brings along any thought of…" (state what it is that you want to work on like prejudice, judgments, hatred, blame, anger, fear, belief in being bad, shame, self-hate, power misuse, misuse of energy, disease, suffering, powerlessness, victimhood, or poverty).

"With my intention as love and forgiveness, I burn the violet flame through every particle and wave of my life energy in every time and place that reflects anything less than what serves my true, positive purpose."

"I trust Source to change every part of me on every single level into the highest level of light and love and abundance and health."

"I ask that I fill my presence with the golden light of love, abundance, and health."

"In my creator's name, I accept this as done. So, it is."

Boat of Wellbeing

Go to a quiet place that you like being, where you can relax fully, and you know you won't be disturbed. Turn off your phone. Get into a comfortable seated or lying position if you can do so without going to sleep.

Make sure that you are comfortable, and then shut your eyes. Focus your attention on your breath. Don't try to do anything to it; just notice it. Your breath is going to change just by focusing on it naturally. Your body and mind will start to relax.

You will likely notice tension being released from your body. You could feel as if you are sinking. Like gravity is pulling you into a sense of relaxation. Continue to focus on your breath. Breathe in. Breathe out. In… and… out.

Take a slow scan across your body to see if you are holding anything inside of your mind or body. There may be something you have been dealing with that comes to mind. You may notice that you have tightness or tension within your body, which means you are grasping or reaching for something.

As you take note of these grasps and stresses, allow them to leave. If you need to attend to something in your life, it can wait and be worked on later. This is a time to relax, to take a little vacation from having to think or plan. If you do notice some stress, don't blame it on anybody else. Notice that it is there, and then allow it to go.

Picture yourself resting on a comfy boat that is floating gently down the river of rejuvenation and love. You can create any type of boat that you want. This boat is being guided by your heart, which has aligned itself with abundance.

The boat has resonated on every level with your pure heart. Everything on the boat is everything that you will need.

When you need something, it will show up in front of you. You have loving companions to take the journey with you. You have all the best food that you will need to nourish yourself. There is music playing that soothes you. Everything on the boat brings you wellbeing and joy.

The only thing you need to do is enjoy yourself and relax and notice everything that you have in your life. Everything is under control. There are no cares or concerns in your life right now because you have everything you need. There is no need to ask for anything. When you notice you need something, it will show up, no matter what it is.

When you notice that you want to do something or fix something, relax and know that it has already been attended to. This is your dream vacation where somebody else is taking care of everything.

There is no need to come up with any plans for how to get things. All you have to do is relax and know that your boat will take you where you need to travel, and it will happen in the best way possible.

Allow yourself to relax because everything is being tended. Focus on the healing and nurturing that is available to you. As you float on down the river, you are being taken further into relaxation and wellbeing. You are filled with clarity and light. Everything good is here. All you have to do is let the river take you into love. Everything is completely handled appropriately.

If stress starts to rise up, don't try to control it. Notice that it's there, and remind yourself that everything is being handled. Relax into the love that surrounds you. Allow your knots to be untangled. Everything is healed. You are at home, nurtured, loved, and appreciated. You are done with work and can relax. You don't have to do anything. Everything is being done for you.

An entire staff of beings is on the boat with you to take care of whatever you need. When you need something, one of these beings appears to help you.

Allow yourself to float along and surrender yourself to a delicious relaxation.

Once you feel ready, you can open your eyes and have a look around. How did it feel? Was it hard for you to let things go and allow other people to take care of the things you needed? If you did, you're not the only person that has that struggle.

Were you able to feel any sense of relief in trusting that you were traveling along the right course that everything had been handled? Were you able to feel the loving energy healing you? This is what you want to reach.

The more you can feel this is you, the higher you will vibrate and the cleaner your chakras will be. The more you vibrate at this level, the healthier and more connected to your true self you will become.

Chakra Healing

This meditation script will bring you along a relaxing trip that will restore and cleanse your chakra's energy. Your entire energy system will retire into a state of balance and harmony.

Let your eyes slowly close. Focus on your breath and allow it to move down through your body, allowing it to relax your belly and soften the mind.

Feel how your seat below you supports you and connects you with the ground beneath you. Allow it to take on your full weight.

Notice all of the sounds that are around you and allow them to be there. Notice the light that you can see through your closed lights. Feel the air that touches your body since the sky that is above and the Earth that stretches out all around you.

Let your mind become empty of anything that you don't need to hold. Let this go away and flow out from you. Let your body release anything that it doesn't currently need. Let this go away and flow out from you.

Pull yourself out of the experiences that you have gone through today. Pull your energies back to your center. Allow yourself to be grounded at the moment.

Start to sense what is around you. Inhale with the energy and notice the rise and fall of your breathing: the way it comes and goes, how it sounds and feels, and its temperature.

Take a deep breath in, all the way down to where your body rests, just below your spine at your root chakra: your belonging. Breathe in here. Allow this space to gently expand and soften. Let it take in nourishment and your energy.

Let you become connected to the ground below you, deep into the depths of the Earth. Bring in the color red. Allow your root chakra to become bathed in this red color, empowering and grounding you. You are in the here and now. Allow your root chakra to take in everything that it needs.

Once you feel ready, let your awareness come to your belly, right below the belly button: your sacral chakra, the center of emotional intelligence, pleasure, and creativity.

Breathe into this space and allow it to expand and soften with your breath. Allow it to take in energy and nourishment. Bring in the color orange. Allow your sacral to be wrapped in this color. Let it feed on the power.

Once you are ready, move on to the area just below your breastbone: your solar plexus, your power.

Breathe into this area and let the solar plexus expand and soften with your breath. Bring in the bright color yellow. Let this sunshine surround your chakra. It will nurture and replenish your chakra. Allow your chakra to take in whatever it needs.

Once you feel ready, move your awareness to the middle of your chest: your heart, your space of love and development.

Breathe gently into your heart and allow it to expand and soften. Bring in the color green into this space. Allow your heart to be surrounded by this nourishment and healing. Allow your heart to consume whatever energy it needs to while you are here.

When the time is right, move your awareness to your neck: your throat, where your will and expression live.

Once you feel ready to return to yourself and become whole — back to the rise and fall of your breathing, back into you — take a breath into your core. To yourself, say, "I am perfect and whole."

Let these words bathe you in their energy. Let it sweep across your spirit, emotions, mind, and body. Take in all the energy that you need.

In your own perfect time, start to notice the air that touches your body. Take note of the sounds that are close and far away.

Take a moment to close down your chakras a bit. Having the intention to do so is enough. Notice the support that you have below you. Notice the way it makes you feel. Support yourself with kindness and love for the unique human being that you are.

Once you feel ready, slowly move your toes and fingers and gently open your eyes.

White Light

Performing this healing meditation regularly will help to increase your self-awareness. This will unlock your ability to heal naturally and will improve your wellbeing. This meditation can be used for yourself and the entire planet as well. This is the perfect way to begin your day.

Begin by sitting in a comfortable chair that fully supports your back and body. Allow your eyes to close. Start to notice your breathing. Don't try to make any changes; just observe how it feels as you breathe in and out with repetition. Do this for a few minutes.

Imagine a stream of white light flowing down for your source and through the top of your head in your crown chakra. This is a glorious waterfall of love, joy, and wellbeing that is coming straight from your creator.

White light shines brightly and shows every color in the rainbow. Every color carries a specific healing power and brings nourishment to every part of your being.

Breathe this stream of light into your crown chakra. This light flows into every cell of your body and brings you enlightenment, and nurtures you.

Breathe this white light through your body until it exits the soles of your feet and spreads deep into Mother Earth.

You are creating a continuous and permanent line of light coming from your source down through your very being into Earth. As you breathe out, you breathe in another dose of this white light and its healing energy, and it goes out to every person in the world.

This beautiful light circulates you. You are free to surrender and let go of everything that ever kept you away from true love. This white light has taken over any old residues of energy. They immediately disappear in their brilliance.

From your crown chakra, you breathe in this perfect light through to your third eye, located in the middle of your forehead. You breathe in pure clarity and love. You release all that has blocked you from receiving the highest amount of love possible.

You ask this healing white light to open up your inner vision to broaden so that your perspective expands.

Through your crown chakra, you breathe in more of this healing light and send it through to your throat chakra living at the base of the throat. This is from where your truth and ability to speak comes. This will release everything that covers your truth.

The light flows out of your energy center and affirms to the world around that you are the highest truth of yourself. When you breathe out, this pure light flows out of your throat chakra out to everybody and brings love and healing to the entire world with your voice.

You release any constricting and separating beliefs that you have stored in this area. You have allowed yourself to become one with the pure light. The white light is now coursing through you and around you.

With every breath you take, this light expands out into a sphere of light that encapsulates your physical body. It includes the alpha and omega chakras that live above and below your body.

Chapter 8: The Energy of Prana

What Is Prana?

Prana is the all-pervading energy that exists inside you and all around you. Many names and terms call it, yet they all refer to the same divine energy: prana. Even some people claim that since prana is everywhere and that it cannot be destroyed, then perhaps prana is God. There are conflicting schools of thought on this matter, but the majority believes that prana only comes from God, but it is not God. Still, prana's nature remains the same: It is everywhere; it is infinite; it cannot be destroyed but is transmuted from one state into another; and that everything — both visible and invisible —

is made of prana. Without prana, then there is no life. From this perspective, it is not hard to say that perhaps prana, indeed, is God. However, this is something that you may have to decide on your own,

How to Control Prana

This is a secret that you must learn to and understand. You will find this extremely helpful, especially when you finally take the actual steps to awaken the Kundalini. When it comes to controlling prana, you should remember that prana follows thought. This means that you can control prana with your mind. But how do you do it? Well, the answer is simpler than you might think. It is through visualization. Yes, you just have to imagine it.

However, this is more than doing a simple imaginary act. You should engage as many senses as possible. For example, if you want to draw prana into your hand, then you can visualize prana, like a flowing river, flowing into your hand. Do not just see it in your mind's eye, but also try to feel it, even hear it and smell it. The more senses are involved, the better it will be. There are, however, two important senses that you should ensure to focus on—the senses of sight (seeing) and feeling.

Again, remember that energy follows thought. To truly engage this energy, you should use visualization. Through visualization, you can effectively direct prana. There are, of course, other ways to control prana, but as far as working on your Kundalini is involved, then the best way to do it is with the use of visualization while you are engaged in meditation.

Do not think of this as a mere exercise with your imagination. You must also have faith that what you visualize is also real. Keep in mind that prana can take any form, color, and shape, and all it takes is for you to control it with your mind.

There is also what is known as tactile visualization. This is also effective. If you find it hard to visualize and "see" things in your mind's eye, you may want to learn tactile visualization instead. Tactile visualization is where you rely solely on your feelings. For example, instead of visualizing the sight of a fire in your hand to produce heat, you can just visualize or imagine your hand getting warmer and warmer, even without having to "see" fire in your hand. However, it should be noted that it is still best to get used to visualization using as many senses as possible. Do not worry if you think you cannot do it in your first few attempts. It may take some practice before you can get used to it, but it is doable, and you can do it.

Here Is a Simple Exercise to Help You Learn to Control Prana

Focus on your hand. You can use either your left or right hand. Now, visualize the energy in your body. You can see it in any way you want. The most common way of visualizing energy is by seeing it as white light. Now, see and feel this energy flow and accumulate in your hand. Keep charging your hand. You can also direct and accumulate energy/Prana in other parts of your body.

Energy is often felt as something warm. Hence, if you accumulate energy in your hand, you may tell if you can do it correctly if you feel that your hand gets warmer. Another sign of energy is when you feel a tingling sensation. This is often felt in the palm of your hand.

Take note that energy is inside you and all around you. The energy inside you is referred to as personal energy. There is also what is known as universal energy. This is the unlimited energy that exists all around you.

Understanding the Nature of Prana

Prana is said to be everywhere. It is inside you and all around you. No life can exist without prana. Prana is also in the breath. Hence, there is a famous practice known as pranayama, which controls one's prana by controlling the breath. Another nature of prana is that it cannot be killed or destroyed. Instead, it can only change or be transmuted from one state into another. It is interesting to note, that conventional science has also proven this teaching, that energy cannot be destroyed; it only changes.

Everything in the universe swims in an ocean of energy. Perhaps this is also how everything is said to be connected. Hence, the web of life.

Prana or energy can also be used for various purposes. It is not just for awakening the Kundalini. Many people use it for healing, such as in reiki and in pranic healing. It can also be used for many other purposes, even for evil. Indeed, prana is everything and everything is composed of prana. Although prana may be seen as one and the same, it should be noted that its quality might vary. When you use prana, only focus on harnessing positive energy.

There are many other ways to direct prana, although the simplest and usual way of doing it is by visualization. Other known ways include dancing, chanting, and certain movements, among others.

Prana is considered important to humans. People with low prana are often more prone to getting sick, while people with lots of prana are more likely to be active and healthy.

Prana or chi has been in existence for centuries; in fact, ancient writings also talked about prana. Mind you, these writings can be traced back to before the time of Christ. However, although prana has been known and used for so long, it is not yet accepted by conventional science. Still, this does not mean that it is not real. Just because science cannot explain something does not mean that it does not exist.

Nadi

All energy is a form of prana, the life force that permeates the world. Prana is the energy behind everything we do, from thought and speech to circulation, digestion, and natural phenomena. There are different subcategories, but our mind and body's systems and actions proceed out of the same energy, prana. Prana flows throw the body along channels called Nadi. The body's principal Nadi is the Sushumna Nadi, which connects all body functions and links our entire physical system. The

Sushumna Nadi is primarily a spiritual energy channel, but it has a physical manifestation and the spinal cord. The spinal cord is thus the main conduit of prana energy through the body.

Along the Sushumna Nadi's length are located six points of particular energy and importance, called chakras. Understanding and controlling these points improves our prana's flow and the function of our bodies and minds, allowing our minds and bodies to work in unity and create spiritual awakening.

While different traditions identify different numbers of minor chakras, most agree that there are seven major ones, all located along the spinal column: the Sahasrara chakra at the crown of the head, which governs wisdom, consciousness, and transcendence of the self; the Ajna or third-eye chakra located in the forehead, which governs clarity, vision, and intuition; the Visuddha chakra in the throat, controlling communication and fluency of thought; the Anahata chakra near the heart, which governs compassion, love, circulation, and balance; the Manipura chakra near the naval or solar plexus, which governs power, fear, growth, and the link between base and higher emotions; the Svadhishthana chakra near the sex organs, which controls joy, pleasure, and relationships; and the Muladhara chakra in the tailbone, which governs instinct, security, and sensuality.

Apart from thousands of years of tradition supporting the idea of the chakras, modern science does too. All seven chakras correspond in location and function to major nerve groupings and important hormonal glands. But the important thing to understand about the chakras is that while they do have physical locations, they are spiritual objects. They are psychic energy with physical expressions. They represent the inextricable link between the physical body, the prana's flow, and the spiritual and conscious realm. All the chakras are vital to emotional well-being and spiritual transcendence, and all represent the harmonious coexistence and unity of the physical and spiritual bodies.

Chapter 9: Third Eye Awakening

When your third eye is fully opened, your wisdom and intuition will come alive. For most people, opening up the third eye chakra is quite challenging, and for some, it could seem just out of reach.

Once you have stimulated your third eye, you will be able to see how your previous decisions have influenced your life and how present decisions will affect your future. You will develop mental flexibility to see the difference between what something seems to be and what it is. With the help of your sixth chakra, you will move past normal abilities. The following strategies will help you to open your third eye chakra.

Get Grounded

The first thing you need to do before you can open your third eye is to have your feet grounded. Also, it's important to go at this slowly and create a good foundation that will give you a good amount of discernment to read your new perceptions with clarity.

Grounding is important because you need to have plenty of energy coursing through your energy system to support a healthy opening. Once you have activated your third eye, the information you get will likely seem unusual and possibly even disturbing.

When you have enough energy and are grounded, you will expand yourself into these new perceptions. This will allow you to avoid common negative side effects of a third eye awakening, like confusion.

Create Silence

You must learn how to have silence in your mind. This can be accomplished through meditation, sitting quietly by yourself, or allowing yourself to be lost in your favorite sport or art.

This helps because your third eye will bring your senses to new levels. Many people will refer to this as "the space in-between" or psychic abilities. To listen to the information that you are sent through your third eye, you have to hear a whisper. If you have a busy mind, you will likely miss your messages.

Focus on Your Intuition

There are lots of different ways to improve your intuition. Since your third eye is your center of wisdom and vision, it helps you know your dreams and what they mean. You may even want to try out lucid dreaming or try reading tarot cards. Find different ways to use your intuition during your day.

Since your third eye is where your higher perception levels live, it helps to be more tuned into your intuition. You don't have to be perfect at intuition. All you need to do is be curious and learn more about intuitive techniques. After some practice, these techniques will become familiar, and you will be confident in your abilities.

The great thing is, there's no need to be serious about it. You can have fun and explore things so that you can keep your chakras open to wonder.

Express Creativity

Allow your creativity to flow by using activities that will allow your imagination to let loose. For example, try learning something new. Don't worry about being perfect either. Allow your inspiration to control your hands, and be open to whatever results you get.

Creativity is a perfect way to allow your rational mind to loosen. All of that mental chatter that tells you that something is wrong or right— and that likes to control every little thing that you do— will be silenced with creativity.

When you can silence this area of your mind and use all of the available possibilities, your third eye will start to blossom.

Chanting

Chanting a mantra will help you to listen to yourself. You can repeat the seed sound for the third eye chakra, AUM, as long as you can keep your focus. You can choose some of the words that I will list below to create your mantra. Pick what works best for you. Repeat them in rhythm with your breath while meditating. You can also repeat them to yourself during the day in a Japa fashion. It should become one with your consciousness.

- SOHAMSO (soe-ha-hm-soe)
- HAMSA (ha-hm-saw)
- VIJNANA (veez-hn-ya-nah)

To help you connect even more with your third eye, you can follow these extra tips. Here are some great ways to improve your intuition and energy:

- Grow psychic awareness
- Practice contemplation
- Work with your spirit guides

- Connect with nature and the elemental energies
- Cultivate curiosity about symbols
- Focus on the space "in-between" things
- Allow your imagination freedom
- Guided meditation
- Visualization
- Dream interpretation and lucid dreaming
- Practice divination
- Strengthen your root and throat chakra
- Allow yourself to be comfortable in silence
- Mediate under the moon
- Practice intuition

The Pineal and Pituitary Gland

If you look up information about the third eye, you will likely start seeing information about the pineal and pituitary glands. Glands and chakras tend to have an intimate relationship because they all represent bodily functions. The pituitary gland is the "master gland" because it is the control of the majority of other glands and the production of hormones.

The pineal gland is found in the middle of your brain and is in line with your eyes. Yogic traditions see this gland as the seat of the soul and as the source of psychic abilities. The pineal gland produces melatonin and regulates our sex maturation and sleep cycle. To help awaken your third eye, you need to nurture your pineal gland. Here's how you can help your pineal gland.

- Take time in complete darkness because it will stimulate the gland and produce what is needed to correct hormones.
- Meditate because it balances the nervous system activities and stimulates various areas of the brain.
- Take supplements, and eat foods that support a healthy pineal gland like tamarind fruit, apple cider, and iodine.
- Get a lot of natural light.

Obstacles

Most people will run into some problems when trying to open their third eye. Here are some of the most common problems:

- They tend to descend consciousness, are conceited.
- Their ego is attached to powers.
- They communicate on the surface.
- They use information about others for their gain.
- They do foolish things.
- They ignore what their body tells them.
- They aren't dreamy.
- They have self-deceiving truths.
- They get distracted by details.
- They listen to others through their concerns.

- They see others as different.
- They are rigidly rational.

If you can overcome these issues and follow the techniques explained above, you will be able to open your third eye, and experience life in a new light

How to Open Third Eye

Keeping the third eye open and energy flow as free-flowing as possible is essential to not only harness your spiritual powers but also to return safely and sanely from those realms beyond human consciousness, a common outcome of Kundalini Awakening. These strategies have known to work magical wonders to open the third eye and keep its energy balanced and unblocked.

Cultivate Silence: Learn to foster the silence of your mind. For an average human, the mind is a cacophony of thoughts and ideas that threaten to take our world by storm. Not only this, but these thoughts also create a lot of noise in our minds. Our ability to hear and interpret the messages that come to us from the higher and subtler realms to get lost in the noise.

The third eye chakra can go to that "in-between" space to collect and get guidance and messages from the other world's spirits. In the presence of noise, you cannot hear the messages. Therefore, you must cultivate silence of the mind and learn to handle overwhelming thoughts.

You can use various ways to calm and silence your mind, including meditation, indulging in your favorite hobby or art, or simply sitting calmly amid nature doing nothing but observing the surrounding beauty.

First, recognize how and when your intuition speaks to you. Usually, intuition is not loud and clear like a human voice. Instead, it sends subtle messages through slow-moving or flashes of imagery. Often, you will talk with your intuition, wondering how to get clarity about the received message.

Sometimes, the messages come in goosebumps, an uncomfortable feeling in the gut, a sour taste in your mouth, or a sense of inexplicable relief. Often, the news could come as an emotion. For example, you intuitively like or hate someone you've just met. This could be your intuition, sending you a message about this person.

Just be alert to subtle forms of messages that your body and mind send you. To do that, you must connect with and talk with your inner voice. With practice, you will realize that you can easily catch on to the subtlest of hints that your intuition is trying to give you.

Try to connect with your intuition daily: Keep aside a dedicated time to connect with your intuition daily. Give time and effort to your intuitive powers and see what they are trying to tell you. This is especially important when you have to make a critical decision. However, to ensure you can understand your intuition's language, you must talk with it every day.

Write down what you felt or experienced when you tried connecting with your intuition. Don't leave it to your memory, at least in the initial stages of your learning experience. Write down what you felt, thoughts, and everything else when you sat down each day and connect with your intuition. The more practice you get, the better your skills will become.

Meditate as often as you can; the deeper your connection is with your intuition, the easier it will be to read and interpret its messages. Meditation is an excellent tool to deepen your relationship with your intuitive powers. Meditation teaches you to clear your mind and recognize the subtle impulses and signs your intuition is trying to give you.

And finally, learn to trust yourself and your intuitive powers. The more faith you have in your powers, the better outcomes you will get. Trust yourself because no one loves you more than you do. No one wants to see you happy and successful more than you do.

Build your creativity skills — each one of us is born with creativity. It is up to us to nurture, nourish and develop it to achieve our full potential. Creativity is a useful tool to eliminate rational fears and crutches that hold you down when you are, in reality, powerful to soar high in the clouds.

When your rational mind is relegated to the background, then the mental chatter also reduces, helping to achieve the calmness needed to communicate with your intuitive powers. When you can calm that part of your mind that wants to take charge of your life, you effectively open up numerous opportunities for yourself. Your third eye chakra has increased space to unfold, grow, and blossom.

Tips to Help Your Creativity Grow and Blossom

Invest your time and energy on hobbies and activities that energize you and make you happy. Learn a new craft or art. It is not important to be perfect in what you do. The trick is to let your inspiration flow through your mind into your hands. Be ready to be surprised when you allow your creativity to flow unhindered.

Experiment with creativity. You need not have a perfect plan. Just do anything that requires your creativity to flow through. For a simple example, just buy yourself an adult coloring book, and experiment with colors. Or make a palette of watercolors and simply splash them around on a piece of paper and observe the results. Or put on some music and dance to it as if no one is looking at you.

Get sufficient nourishment for your body through nutritious food, restful sleep, and a good amount of physical activity.

Invest in yourself. Do something once a week that is only for you. It could be something as simple as a visit to the local art gallery or sipping a cup of morning tea by yourself, or an afternoon curled up in bed with your favorite book, or anything else. This alone time will give you a deep sense of calm and allow you to connect with yourself and your intuitive powers.

Spend some time with nature. Take a walk in the park. Or take a hike to a place close to your home. Look for and find an opportunity to spend time with nature.

Ground Yourself to Soar Fearlessly*:* It is an ironic truth that we must plant both our feet firmly on the ground to soar fearlessly. In the same way, to open our third eye, our root chakra should be strong and robust, giving you the needed sense of stability and strength with the support you can soar fearlessly. Your root chakra forms the firm foundation over which you can build your life that takes you on wondrous flights outside the human realm. The root chakra is what brings you back home.

Also, the information that comes into our body and mind when our third eye is opened could be unfamiliar, unusual, and difficult to digest for common minds. Therefore, you must first energize and empower your tangible body and mind, and only when you are ready can you tackle the power of the subtle universe.

The Third Eye Meditation

Any time that meditation is used, it is to bring about a particular state of mind. Some people meditate to bring themselves to a clearer state of mind, while others try to use it for relaxation. Among the many ways that meditation can be used is for activating the third eye.

If you look through history at the Taoists, Buddhists, and other cultures that have emphasized opening the third eye, you will notice that meditation is a common practice. This is because meditation helps bring the mind to that state where it is focused but relaxed. Meditation has the potential to bring the third eye into focus, activating it in a way that has not yet been activated in your lifetime.

Choosing the Right Posture for Meditation

If you look to different cultures where yoga or meditation is practiced, you will emphasize posture. This is not necessarily to promote the idea of relaxation or meditation but to help align the energy centers at the spine. When you meditate, especially with the third eye, you want the chakras to be aligned and energized.

The spine is the center of the body. It is a bundle of nerves and tissue that travels between your brain and the rest of your body, giving you the connection you need to move around and accomplish things. The spine is the root of the nervous system and provides the basic structure of our body. Many cultures also say that it holds the soul's potential because of the DNA and RNA molecules within. These DNA and RNA molecules contain the codes that determine our potential in life.

While you should aim to keep the spine straight and aligned while meditating, you should do it comfortably. If you are rigid and in pain, it will be quite difficult to focus on your meditation. It will also feel unpleasant and unnatural, taking your mind away from the natural experience you are trying to create while opening the third eye.

The most traditional position involves sitting on your buttocks with your legs crossed. You can also tuck your feet under your body by sitting straight up with your buttocks on your feet. Some other variations include lying down, sitting, or standing. What truly matters is your comfort and proper alignment of the spine.

Meditative Practices to Open the Third Eye

More than one type of meditation can induce the trance-like state that can open the third eye. The meditative practice that you use ultimately depends on you and the way that your brain is wired. Even though meditation is known for helping activate the third eye, not everyone can meditate the same way and have the same experience. This section will go over several variations of meditation that can help you activate the third eye.

Basic Third Eye Meditation

This is the most basic of the third eye meditations. It works best while lying down in a quiet room. It can be light or dark; whichever will be the least distracting. Before you sink into the attempt to open the third eye, start by closing your eyes and releasing all the worries from your day. Breathe in and out, imagining that you are exhaling all your pains and stresses.

As you feel the worries float away, turn your attention to the spot where the third eye is located, on the center of your forehead. Do not look at it through your physical eyes, but through your mind's eye. As you feel and see this spot in your mental image, picture yourself opening this eye. It will feel strange and be difficult at first, but it is important to be persistent. Some people see a strong "light" once they open the eye, but not everyone reports this. Focus your intent on opening this eye and let whatever happens to happen.

Mirror Meditation

For people who have trouble visualizing their third eye's brightness, meditating in front of a mirror can help them achieve an open state. Sit in a traditional meditation pose or sit straight up in a chair with your feet on the floor. You want to have a mirror across from you, where you can see your face and upper body.

To meditate, start by inhaling to a count of four and then exhaling to four. Pay attention to detail as you breathe in and out—you should feel your stomach expand and contract fully. After several breaths, you will develop lightness in your head—the increase in oxygen causes this.

As you focus on your breaths, you will notice that intrusive thoughts are fading away. When your mind is clear, turn your focus to the point where the third eye sits, just between the eyebrows and under the surface of the forehead. Look at yourself in the mirror and imagine a bluestone or circle on your forehead. Visualize this stone glowing with blue or indigo light—this is the third eye transforming into an activated energy center.

Progressive Third Eye Chakra Meditation

For each step of this progressive meditation, you will focus your attention on each point below for three to five minutes each. You will also focus on the third eye's feelings and the third eye's relationship and awareness as you focus on each area. You can sit upright or cross-legged as you focus, depending on what is most comfortable. As you tune your focus to each area, you will want to monitor it non-judgmentally, simply experiencing it without trying to control it too much.

First, you are going to hone in on your sense of existence in the present time. Focus on the following things one at a time:

- The sensations from the environment around you, like a gently blowing wind or the way that the pillow/chair feels beneath you
- The sensations from your body, the way that your body moves as you breathe and the way your heartbeat feels, as well as the awareness of the pressure of your third eye
- The emotions that are coursing through your body and mind
- The thoughts that result from these emotions and how you are thinking
- The “I am” statements that you are experiencing, for example, thinking “I am strong” or “I am capable” vs. “I am stupid” or “I am unable to do anything right”

- Impressions and memories coming from the subconscious, in response to your thought and emotional patterns
- The present time and how it is being recorded into your memory for future use

Once you have dedicated awareness to all these areas of your present existence, it will be time to turn your focus to the chakras, and eventually, the third eye. Starting at the base of your spine, spend the same 3–5 minutes focusing on each of the chakras. Move from your spine's base to the spot behind the navel, then up to the solar plexus. From here, you are going to give your attention to the heart chakra and the throat chakra before moving up to the third eye chakra.

Keep your eyes closed as you turn your focus inward, bringing your attention to the consciousness within. Spend as long as you want in this state of consciousness. When you are ready to return to your normal state of awareness, spend a minute or two in each of the states that brought you into your third eye meditation. Move through the chakras and then focus on your present state of awareness in the world. This will help ground you, bringing a sense of calm and peace as you step into the world of awareness.

Object Third Eye Meditation

All our lives, we are taught to adjust our perception of the world according to what we see with our physical eyes. As you start to practice third eye meditation, you may find it difficult to close the physical eyes and focus on nothingness.

One way to help you sink into the proper state of mind is to use a physical, free-form object to focus your intention. Crystal balls or spheres are a good choice, as are candles.

Mystics have used spherical shapes made of crystal for centuries to practice their craft. The science behind this is in the crystal's shape and molecular structure, which does not have a real pattern. As you gaze into it, its lack of patterns lets it search for energies and patterns. It forces you to look into yourself and search for what you are looking for because it cannot have anything imprinted on it by the physical world around the sphere.

Candles are another free-form shape ideal as a focal point during meditation. This is especially true since fire can be viewed as a type of energy. The fixed gaze can be used on any object, but a candle makes a great fixed point. It is called Trataka. When you sit to candle gaze, you should focus your attention on a room with low lighting. Place a candle on a surface that is close to eye level, so it is almost right in front of you. Breathe deeply as you bring your attention to the candle's flame and hold it in your gaze.

Chapter 10: The Power and Benefits of an Open Third Eye

Opening the third eye is something that will take a great deal of time and focus. Any person can indeed tap into the power of the third eye and experience the effects that it can have on their life. However, not every person is going to have the motivation to work toward this goal. Opening the third eye takes perseverance and time. This section will help you understand what you are gaining as you open the third eye to have a clearer picture of what you are working toward.

You Open Your Mind to the Possibilities around You

Principles like the law of attraction focus on how the energy that you put out determines what you receive in life. When you open your third eye, you will start to unlock the world around you in new ways. Instead of seeing the obstacles in your way, you will learn to identify problems and see patterns that lead you to the future that you want.

One of the biggest reasons people do not achieve success or get the things they want in life is limiting their options. They may shy away from certain situations because of past incidents or are just unsure of what they need to take to put their goals into action. When you access the power of the third eye, you are accessing the potential of the world around you. Your soul is no longer asleep—it is ready to work with your active mind to achieve your most grandiose dreams.

You Can Form Your Own Opinions

Have you ever met someone that would not sway their opinion about something, regardless of the facts that were presented to them? This happens when people are obsessed with the idea of being seen as "right." They often go along with the most popular opinion and refute anything that does not support it. Unfortunately, that is how people end up turning a blind eye to all the inequalities and injustices in the world around them.

Once you have opened the third eye, you will find yourself thinking in a whole new. The thoughts you have will be more critical, allowing you to ask questions and evaluate all the information available before forming an opinion or making a decision.

Your Spirit Awakens

Have you ever heard the word sheeple? This term is usually used to describe people who blindly follow, be it politics, religion, the media, or something else. They are not the critical thinkers of the world—they simply do and think what is expected of them. Once you open your third eye, you start to understand the reality of the world around you. Do not be surprised if you see that the world is a dark place—it is brimming with authoritative figures that work others like puppets. Inequalities and injustices exist everywhere. However, as you uncover this, know that there are also beautiful places in the world. Your motivations and goals may change as you open the third eye because you will be moved toward a more accessible lifestyle, where you can experience more profound compassion, truth, and love.

Your Sleep Will Improve

One of the pineal gland functions is to govern sleep and wake cycles, which means you will sleep better after opening your third eye. Many people also experience more vivid dreams. Over time, you will start to learn that the realm of dreams is truly unlimited by the possibilities. The possibilities will continue to increase as you realize the immensity of your spiritual self.

You Could Learn to Astral Travel

People who completely access the third eye sometimes learn to astral travel. As you realize that there are limitless possibilities and that your spiritual self is not necessarily connected to your physical body, it will become apparent that you do not have to be limited by your existence in the physical world. Time and space are not definite, fixed elements in your life unless you allow them to consume you. Some people experience this as the ability of their soul to leave their body, traveling to any time and place in the universe.

You Will Gain a Deeper Intuition

Some people experience an extreme sense of intuition after opening the third eye, which is often referred to as a sixth sense. Some people have natural psychic powers that are buried deep within them. These powers come from tapping into the instinctual signals that are being sent from the world around them. This speaks a lot to the proverbial saying that "all you need to know is already contained within." You can learn the secrets of the world by expanding your consciousness and turning your focus inward.

You Will Develop a Deeper Sense of What You Want

It is incredibly easy to be distracted by the material pull of the world around us. Advertisements are everywhere, telling us the things that we "need" to be happy. The idea of success is often pushed as making as much money as possible, even more money than you could ever need in a lifetime. The problem with this is that it leaves a lot of people unhappy, unsure of what goals they should be striving for to achieve that "dream" that has been promised to many.

Upon opening your third eye, you will notice that the desires and material gains of the world around you do not seem quite as important. You'll gain a deeper insight into what you want in life that will make you happy, as well as the path that you must take to get there.

You'll Experience Heightened Creativity

People who are limited by their physical existence in the world often hold themselves back because of the guidelines and judgments from the world around them. It is easy for people to feel as if others are critical of their creative work since creativity cannot be mandated or regulated. When you open the third eye, you are no longer bound to the strict lines of the world around you. You gain the confidence to take on your creative projects and bring them into reality.

Stress Will Melt away

Awakening the third eye shifts your feeling of consciousness inward, so the things going on in the world around you are not as significant. This reduced level of stress and anxiety may realize that the small occurrences in the world mean less in the grand scheme of things. When you are connected to everything around you, it gives you greater control over the things that are stressing you out, and you develop the ability to make a greater, more positive impact in your own life.

The third eye also gives you insight into how you can make stresses melt away. Instead of focusing on the stress and anxiety, you will find your mind is open to solutions and that each day, you wake up determined to work toward your goals and remove the stressors from your life.

Improved Overall Life

The bottom line is that when the third eye is awakened, you are inviting the things that you need for success into your life. You gain a deeper insight into your goals, achieving happiness, and stress reduction. Your quality of relationships with yourself and others will improve, and you will experience better sleep, heightened creativity, and possibly even experience certain powers like foresight, astral projection, or seeing auras. All these things will come together to help you achieve a better quality of life so that you can start living in the way you were intended to.

Chapter 11: Prepare Body and Mind for Kundalini Awakening

Now that you have a greater understanding of the chakras and how Kundalini plays such an important part in the vibration and balancing of each chakra, you can now put some of these ideas into practice. If you are reading this book, you are undoubtedly curious about how to begin such a journey. Keep in mind that this book gives a general overview of Kundalini energy and the process of awakening, but if you want to go deeper into the journey, don't hesitate to read more about it, take some yoga classes, and even connect with a Yogi or Guru, or a community of people who are on a similar journey, or who have experienced this awakening in their own life. Remember, awakening the Kundalini energy may be universal, but the experience will be unique to you, so stay positive and open-minded during the rising of your divine life-force.

Preparations for the Mind, Body, and Spirit

There isn't just one way your dormant energy becomes awakened. It can vary significantly from person to person. Some people practice yoga and meditation for years, working with Gurus before anything happens. For others, it can be completely spontaneous and caused by a buildup of traumatic situations, addictions or significant loss or grief, whether or not the person has any previous knowledge of what Kundalini even is. There are plenty of stories like these, which is why it's important to remain open-minded with yourself and all the other human souls looking for answers or enlightenment.

If you decided to read this book, you have already begun this journey. Knowing more about it can help you feel more aware of what is potentially ahead for you or even someone you know.

Preparing your mind, your body, and your spirit can be a great way to begin. Even if you have already experienced some of these things, this book can be a great resource for staying in balance or becoming more involved with the journey instead of letting it naturally unfold without any guidance or practice. Sometimes, when you let it unravel naturally and don't practice any energy work, yoga, meditation, or other balancing or healing practices, the experience can feel more chaotic and uncomfortable, more disorienting and unpredictable.

Finding ways to nurture yourself through awakening is key to a joyful and fully opening experience.

Each fundamental part of yourself can go through some preparations to allow for a more intentional awakening. Like you read before, it can happen spontaneously for some people, but chances are, if you are reading this book, you are interested in and excited about starting that process of awakening your Kundalini and knowing your divine truth.

Below are a few simple ways you can prepare your mind, body, and spirit to awaken.

Mind

You can always invent your own mantras to suit your needs better, but try to find ways to speak to yourself with the language and frequency of love. Say mantras first thing in the morning before work, while sitting in traffic, before bed, or any other time that feels appropriate.

Start practicing simple meditations, especially if you have never meditated before. Try not to overthink meditation. The point is to clear the mind of thought, but if the thoughts come, let them and then see them pass away from you like an ocean wave or a cloud. You can even find guided meditations online if you are not ready to guide yourself. Just search "guided meditation" and find what feels right for you.

Body

Exercise. You don't need to join a gym or lift weights. You don't need to take aerobics classes or run 10 miles. Go for a walk around your neighborhood. Dance to a song you like in your living room—Tread water in a swimming pool. Go for a hike on the trail. Just move your body in some way that feels pleasant, that doesn't feel like work, and that simply allows you time to get your blood flowing.

Stretch. You don't have to stretch every day, but a couple of times a week is very beneficial. You can practice yoga poses or find a wide variety of places to find stretching routines online, in books, or in a dance class at a studio. One thing to keep in mind when you stretch: it is best to hold each stretch for a minute to a minute and a half. Your body needs the time actually to experience the result of the stretch. If you only do it for ten seconds, there won't be much of a change in your muscles and tissues.

Eat well. Diet has a great impact on the way we feel and our energy. As part of Kundalini awakening, you may have a natural inclination to change your diet, which has been commonly reported. If you don't already and prepare for the experience ahead, start eating well by avoiding processed foods, alcohol, sugar, and large quantities of caffeine. Take it a step at a time if it's too much to do all at once. Eat more whole foods, vegetables, fruits, grains, lean meats, seeds. Drink a lot of water. Switch to tea instead of coffee. All of this will start preparing your body for the adventure ahead.

Spirit

Adopt a self-care practice. There are so many ways to do this. You can take a sunbathe in the morning light and soak in the warmth and glow, focusing on your energy channels and how they feel as you relax. Draw a hot bath and add Epsom salt, preferred essential oils, and candlelight, and spend quality time in the water letting your muscles soak. Lean up against your favorite tree with your favorite book and your favorite snack for as long as you want. These are a few examples to try or create your own ideas that resonate with who you are. The goal is to give yourself permission to love and care for yourself.

Keep a dream journal. The subconscious mind communicates so much to us when we sleep. In ascension, as the Kundalini rises, many people report having very profound dreams, premonitions, contact with spirit guides, or astral travel experiences. Start keeping a dream journal to begin communicating with your dream world and your higher consciousness and look for messages from within.

Start a gratitude practice. It is proven that expressing gratitude, whether it is vocal, written down, or in mind, can positively change your vibration frequency. The concept of gratitude is a part of living as an enlightened human being. You can keep it simple. Begin by saying or writing things like, "I am grateful to have shelter and food to eat." "I have gratitude for the job I have right now." "I am thankful to be a part of this world." And so on. The great thing is, it can be about anyone and anything. The point is that thankfulness and appreciation is a valuable practice that brings you into closer alignment with your divine power and ultimate transcendence.

Start practicing these things today! It will be a helpful way for you to prepare for the quality of life you are looking for as you seek awakening.

Chapter 12: Diet for Kundalini

Believe it or not, your diet has a major impact on Kundalini energy. What you fuel your body with is a form of energy in and of itself. Not only does it provide you with physical energy, but it also works together with your aura and other non-physical energy. It truly does impact you on many different levels. If you want to have a powerful impact on your Kundalini and support it in the best way possible, be sure to pay attention to your diet and what you are eating.

Avoid eating two to three hours before you plan on doing your kriyas and asanas. Since this yoga uses many different body locks, breathing exercises, vigorous movements, and asanas, you may feel extremely uncomfortable if you are doing so on a full stomach. If you feel you lack energy, have an energy bar beforehand.

Most yoga practices recommend consuming a Sattvic diet, which promotes clarity and calmness, instead of rajasic or tamasic diets; because of the energetic and physical nature of this yoga, consuming some rajasic food isn't that big of a deal. Rajasic foods promote activity. It's still recommended that most of your diet be sattvic. These include fresh and sweet foods like nuts, vegetables, fruit, etc. Rajasic foods are spicier and stimulate, like tea, fish, eggs, garlic, onions, etc. Tamasic foods are meats, stale foods, fatty foods, and so on.

It's important to drink plenty of water after practicing a kriya because it is designed to get your vessels, nerves, tissues, and organs to release toxins. Water will help you cleanse out the toxins.

Adjusting Your Diet for Kundalini Awakening

Many people believe that to promote a healthy spiritual flow, you need to eat a vegetarian or vegan diet. With Kundalini, this is not believed to be necessary. However, it is important that you learn to adjust your diet to suit your body's changing needs. As your spiritual energy changes, your physical body will typically desire to change what it consumes as well.

Those who are awakening or who have awakened already tend to avoid eating any foods that introduce unhealthy energies into the body.

Common things that you will likely feel naturally drawn to avoid when you are awakening include things like: alcohol, recreational drugs, red meat, sugar, and excessive chemicals such as the preservatives they put in convenience meals. You may begin to find yourself wanting or even craving more water, whole organic foods like vegetables and fruits, fish and poultry, or otherwise. Some people may even find themselves naturally drawn to releasing meats of all varieties and instead pursue a vegetarian or vegan diet. That is perfectly fine, too. The idea here is to listen to your body and what your body wants instead of trying to eat a diet that has been manufactured for you by someone else. Only you know what you need. Following these natural requests from your body will greatly impact your ability to feel your best and allow your Kundalini energy to flow fluidly.

Listening to Your Body

Your body is already well aware of what it needs to survive and thrive. As you are right now, your body has likely been consuming foods that would keep it comfortable amidst a high-stress lifestyle that may have involved many difficult or painful emotions. This is natural, especially in the Western world, where emotional self-care is less popular than in other cultures worldwide.

Learning to listen to your body takes some time. Additionally, you may find yourself realizing that as you awaken more, your body needs to change.

They may even change beyond diet, encouraging you to exercise differently, use different body care products, or even rest at different times. Being able to really tune into what your body needs is a powerful practice that can truly help you so much in your awakening.

As you grow used to communicating with your body, recognizing what it needs and what it no longer wants becomes significantly easier. You can begin to intuitively recognize anytime something is causing your body to feel sluggish, slow, or otherwise "off." You can also begin to recognize anytime your body feels empowered, high energy, and positive. Naturally, you will want to begin practicing more of what makes you feel good and less of what does not. This is how you can intuitively support your body and begin using diet, exercise, and overall physical wellbeing to promote and support your Kundalini awakening and balancing.

Ayurveda Diet and Kundalini

One form of diet that regularly finds itself incorporated in Kundalini awakening and energy is Ayurveda. Ayurveda is a traditional Hindu system of medicine that uses diet, herbs, and yogic breathing to promote physical, mental, and spiritual wellbeing.

Seeing a professional Ayurvedic practitioner who can assess your unique body type and provide you with advice on how to balance your energies through diet can be powerful. This practice can help you use your diet as a tool to awaken your energies further and thrive, allowing you to feel your best as often as possible. It is a highly recommended tool to use when performing your Kundalini awakening, even when you are balancing your energies.

Dietary Restrictions and Purification Exercises

Part of bringing your physical body into balance is being conscientious about what you put into it. There's no one correct diet for following Kundalini yoga—the point of dietary restrictions is to eat moderate amounts of simple, healthy, nourishing food that will support your body without overstimulating or punishing it. Different teachers have different opinions but agree that aspirants ought to adjust and perfect their diets depending on their own bodies' needs. Typically, simple foods like milk, fruit, lentils, nuts, and vegetables are recommended, while meat, salt, alcohol, and strongly flavored foods are forbidden. Eat only as much as you need to, and make your meals simple and regular. Attachment to food only creates more attachments to the particulars of the earthly world, making the transcendence of it impossible—you can't negate your individuality if you're craving something particular. Overeating also makes the body sluggish and less responsive to hatha yoga training.

Also, as a preliminary to the strict exercises involved in Kundalini awakening, traditionally aspirants practice various bodily purification exercises involving the digestive tract, sinuses, lungs, and other body parts. These practices are an important part of preparing the body for the strenuous process of kundalini awakening.

Chapter 13: How to Awakens Kundalini Energy

Now that you understand that your Kundalini is a reservoir of spiritual energy and gives you aliveness, purpose, and passion, let's look at how you can begin to awaken this energy. Kundalini is probably the most sensual energy you could ever imagine.

Once you go through a Kundalini awakening, you feel as if you have been healed. You will have the feeling of being able to change anything and everything that is in your life. You will have access to an unlimited well of energy, knowledge, and the sensation that your soul won't die.

One of the most interesting aspects of a Kundalini awakening is what will happen when it works into relationships with other people. You will be able to connect, love, and trust them purely because the higher intelligence is found everywhere. You will be able to let go of judgments, get rid of any existing blocks, drop any resistance to love and fear of intimacy. Once your mind is consumed with the Kundalini energy, you will feel amazing and powerful because it clears away everything that blocks you from being your true self with others.

With the awakening, you will drop that veil that prevents you from seeing the truth of the world. You will enter a world to your spiritual self, true love, abundance, and become one with the Divine in everything around you. As the Kundalini awakens, it will move up your spine. It can feel warm or tingling. These sensations are the energy purifying you and will bring you to the highest conscious state.

You will receive an expanded energy state, blissful love, and cosmic thinking. You will comprehend reality, and you will know what complete freedom from suffering is like and the possibility for enlightenment. You will constantly feel happy, and everything you do, your choices, will always be the best.

One of the best aspects of awakening your Kundalini is the healing energy that you will receive. You will soon be able to heal yourself and others that are willing and open. Kundalini's power is fierce, and it has no limitations. The energy you will have coursing through you will be contagious to everybody who comes in contact with you. People around you will leave feeling freer, happier, and higher. By being yourself, you will naturally enlighten the world around you. This is something that you can get thrilled about.

An essential part of experiencing a full awakening is how committed you are to your spiritual path. How devoted are you to seeing and feeling the divine that lives in everything and everyone? How much do you want to let in trust and get rid of doubt? A good way of figuring out how devoted you .are is to see how you feel around people that typically make you suffer. If you are devoted to something, you will practice compassion towards everybody, even those that cause you pain. You can relax your body which is what Kundalini needs to be able to move. When you are devoted to relaxing in this connection, you will naturally connect with the universe and awaken your Kundalini.

It's a good thing to know that Kundalini lives within you; all you have to do is wake it up. If you were to wake her up without knowing the proper way to do so, you might end up disrupting your typical reality. This can end up being negative or positive; it all depends on how you perceive it. If you have the correct foundation, you will have a rather enjoyable experience.

To start your awakening journey, begin by practicing a special Kundalini meditation every day. There are several ways to awaken your Kundalini, but the most popular is to breathe in a golden light up and down your spine as much as you can all day. This can be done when you are watching TV, resting, eating, cooking, standing in line, driving, and doing it anytime because you are constantly breathing.

It's important to know that this awakening can be the best thing that has ever happened to you if you are fully devoted, or it can be the worst that has ever happened because you aren't fully devoted. It depends on how you look at it; is it "for you" or "to you." This type of paradigm shift will depend on your attachment to your ego.

When you are able to take that step past your ego is the biggest part of opening all the doors in you for Kundalini to flow. To get rid of your ego, you have to honor this: you're an infinite soul that can never die. You have to believe that you are not just a physical body truly, instead, you have a spiritual immortal. Perspective is an important part of being able to handle Kundalini rushing through you. The more inclusive you are in your perspective of your spiritual being, the easier it will become for you to accept the energy of Kundalini.

Two more factors play into being able to awaken your Kundalini. First, how sensually and sexually open you are. Second, how open you are to a spiritual transformation. If you have an open sensual and sexual energy flow with the source, then the pathway is already paved to receive Kundalini's energy. This doesn't just mean your sex center, but every center that lives up your spine. The bottom three, solar plexus down, is the foundation you need to build. It needs to be relaxed and solid for your Kundalini to rise up through.

When you awaken your Kundalini it can feel like you have tapped into a million watts while your body can only hold 100 watts. This is why you need to prepare yourself to be able to accept a million watts with ease easily. Daily meditation can help you to receive all of this energy. Your body will become opened enough to be able to receive this healing energy from the universe.

This is a lifelong commitment, so start today. Begin by loving how your life is at this moment and start being aware, awake, and living in the moment. Treat your body gently and love it as it is. Listen to yourself and give it what it needs. This includes have a good diet, bathing, exercising, and treating it like it's sacred. There are likely several mental and emotional blocks within your body attached to your ego that causes some limiting beliefs. These blocks will interfere with your awakening.

Definitely do not try to force your awakening. If you try to push it through any sexual blocks, you will likely experience pain. This is telling you to stop and work on emotional healing. Pain is the body's way of telling you to slow down, listen, be silent, heal and relax. Be gentle with yourself and continue to do your daily practices. You will end up having better health, energy, and sex.

When you open your Kundalini, you will find creative energy, and you will want to become more conscious, alive, and healed. This will make your life full of more joy, love, and gratitude than you have ever felt before.

It's important to know that the universe will never give you anything that you cannot handle or that you need on some level. If you have a severely blocked Kundalini and you find that sex is painful, this pain means that you have trauma locked within the cells and wounds trying to be fixed. BE GENTLE! The golden rule of Kundalini awakening is, be gentle and heal your wounds.

You will find many people say that awakening makes you go crazy or that there is a ton of energy and that you feel out of control; this is just your ego falling away. Kundalini is a fire that will burn away your ego, and you will become liberated to follow your spiritual path. This is how you become purified from suffering in the past, present, and future. That's what makes Kundalini so amazing.

Opening your heart to love is a secret to experiencing a blissful awakening. When you have love, everything you experience is fantastic. Ease yourself into meditation and allow love to guide you.

Your ego is what makes you want instant gratification and results. That's why it's hard to stick with a weight loss regimen because you want it to work overnight. If you allow your ego to rule your awakening, you will only cause a delay in your awakening. If you are entirely and truly devoted to your spiritual focus, then you will have a connection to love, and then all you have to do is surrender to it.

Your Kundalini energy wants to be able to travel up your spine and through your head to give you a direct connection to the divine. It's designed this way to carve your spiritual path so you can see where you need to travel. By performing a simple Kundalini meditation, you will automatically feel an energy expansion and cause tingling sensations in your spine that will give you enjoyable energy waves.

Making a choice to go through an awakening is one of the best gifts you can give yourself. You will be able to enjoy life a lot more. Each sight, touch, smell, and taste will have a deeper connection than ever before. It is a higher level of living.

Tips for Your Awakening Process

Whether performed through spiritual discipline or by accident, the awakening process can cause challenges for you. It's like your body has been amped to 110–220 wiring, and as the appliance, you haven't learned how to adapt your body to it. It is very rare for you to go through an awakening before you have completed months and possibly years of the clearing.

This energy's goal is to bring you together with your universal self, non-self, or the peace passed through understanding. Some scripture refers to Kundalini as a goddess; they called her Shakti, which can awaken and runs through the body through the head's top to connect with the God Shiva, her lover. This represents universal consciousness.

During this journey, your self-identification, illusions, and beliefs related to your current personality are dissolved away. You may end up feeling like you don't belong in this world. You are instead moving towards a vastness of the entire world.

The clearing is said to be a purification process, or, according to the Hindu, you will release your samskaras and vrittis. Samskaras refers to the need to work out problems for past lives or the consequences of things that have happened in your present life. Vrittis refers to the movement of your thoughts and mind. Several practices work to overcome and calm the vrittis activity.

You are a spirit that lives in a physical body. Your body cells are similar to a hologram and contain memories from everything that has ever happened to you. When the energy moves through and transforms the body, the areas with contractions, memory, pain, or energy react to the change. This is when you will have feelings of rushes, vibrations, heat, jerking, pain, and other such phenomena during an awakening. Sometimes, these movements are associated with a chakra as it is opened, which is just another way of saying that new possibilities will emerge as pain is released.

Each person deals and carries their pain in several different ways, just like you live your life in a way different than mine, and so there are several different ways to respond to the new energy. If you suffer from an old injury's physical problems, you may notice that area to be extra sensitive. If you consume an unhealthy diet, or your lifestyle puts you in toxic emotional energy, this can cause you to be more susceptible to difficulties. If you have suffered any kind of abuse or have a history of drug use or alcoholism, your body may be hard to awaken because it tries to clear out all memories. If you tend to fight against things and like to have full control, you will find that the process is a lot hard because of your resistance.

For the aforementioned possible problems, here are some types to help you ease through your awakening process so that you can find and live with inner peace.

You may feel the energy as intense and coarse, but it’s very rarely painful. Typically fear and trying to stop it will be the cause of the pain. If you experience a lot of bodily movement, lay down a couple of times during the day and allow the energy to spread throughout you, and remove the blockages that don’t belong to you and what needs to be released moment in time. This typically takes about 20 minutes, and then you will be able to relax. This needs to be done if you work where you are more exposed to negative energy or pain from others like therapeutic or healing work or work where there is a lot of alcohol consumed or in hospitals. If you continue to have constant physical pain, it may be in your best interest to be medically evaluated.

Find out what it is your body wants to eat. Often, you will find that you need a major dietary shift like eating smaller meals, avoiding red meat, going on a plant-based diet, and giving up alcohol and drugs. If you struggle with a persistent problem with your energy, start doing detective work to figure out what it is that can be causing your problem. How long has it been since you last ate, and what did you consume? Would some bread or protein help to calm down the problem? Maybe some herbal tea or burdock root? Yogis recommend warm almond milk and ghee with some sugar, no honey, to help calm heat and energy.

Pay attention to your belly and heart and not so much in your head. Use practices that help to center you into the present. The best options are devotional practices like heart-centered meditation or chanting. These help to open you to experience your deeper self, the eternal self. Start creating more connections with other people. It's also a good idea to start volunteering either for nature or animal organizations; this can help your awakening to be more balanced. You may even find it comforting to call upon an image of an ally like a symbol, saint, teacher, goddess, or god. You can also imagine a golden light surrounding you. Some have found success in talking to Kundalini as a Goddess. These are different types of archetypal energies that can help your psyche as it travels through several challenges during your change.

Practice things that help you to be more open. Things like long walks, movement processes, acupressure, dance, Tai Chi, yoga, or anything else that you find yourself drawn to. If you're not sure of what fits you best, start experimenting and find what feels best to you. Your body is what carries you and grounds your spirit. No matter how realized you are, you will be living in your body for many years to come. The more you take care of it, the better options you will have to express your realizations. Somebody who is sick or dying can be a complete and beautiful expression of the divine as much as a healthy person. Poor health does not keep you from being able to be enlightened. People who have sat with the dying have said that more light will shine through as earthy attachments let go. You should not see this as advocacy for asceticism. While you are alive, having a flexible and open body can accomplish the same thing and without all the distraction and pain. It's also useless to discipline your body by overdoing physical activity. You have to find that midline that brings together the body and the spirit.

Know when you wake up that you don't know what will happen and be excited to find out things as they happen. Instead of constantly being in control and worrying about things, just be present at the moment and be ready for whatever may come up to handle it the best you can. The things that happen during an awakening will be completely unpredictable and will pass, as long as you simply notice them, and you don't try to control it or fight it.

You will sometimes experience psychic openings, energetic swings, emotional swings, and several other shifts that will be unfamiliar to you. Just observe what happens. Don't think you have to fix these changes. This will eventually pass.

Suppose you ever experienced any serious trauma in your past and you didn't go through therapy. In that case, it'd be extremely useful to release any pain you have associated with these memories that may come up. People that successfully went through good therapy before they started their awakenings didn't have as many difficulties. Therapy gives you the skills to express, witness, and release so that you can move past the problem. The therapist doesn't have to understand what Kundalini is, as long as they accept that it is part of the process you are going through. What you are more interested in then is to learn how to release emotions related to your past. Ensure that you find a compassionate and experienced therapist and view your spirituality as support and motivation to work through your healing.

Stop being around people and places that create pain in your life. You will probably become more sensitive when you awaken your Kundalini. You will find it harder to handle the energy in large discount stores, nightclubs, or competitive and tense family gatherings. It is perfectly okay to put yourself first and create extra quiet time, more close friendships, and possibly a new job if you find the old one becoming more stressful. You don't ever have to prove anything by making yourself do things you don't want to do. You have to rediscover who you are and what makes you comfortable and what feels natural. Live authentically. You may realize you have new creative needs, which gives you a wonderful chance to express yourself. Garden, paint, sculpt, dance, write, draw, any of these are perfect ways to nurture yourself and ease your way through the psychic changes.

Get yourself an awakened teacher to spend time with. For most, meditation will become a very intrinsic part of your life. The awakened teacher can help to convey peace to you and allow you to sit in your true nature's silence. Your awakened teacher can have a sort of spiritual persuasion or none at all. They don't even have to be interested in Kundalini. The important thing is that they show compassion and tolerance for everybody that they work with. You will learn the art of being able to sit and be and you will discover the cure for the suffering in your life. With some time you will find the complaints of the body and mental activity will just fall away and you will find a deep understanding to arise. This will give you a sense of invitation, freshness, openness, and completion of your greater self's expression. Once you have completed your awakening you will no longer have any doubt that it was the right thing. Where you will go from there, you won't know. You will just surrender to change.

Chapter 14: The Effects of Kundalini Activation on the Body, Emotions, and Mind

Procrastinating Getting Started with a Daily Meditation Routine

It's very common for people, even those with a great interest in chakra healing and energy, to begin meditating and then trail off, letting their routine fall by the wayside. In this way, meditation is just like exercise. It's easy to go to the library and read every fitness book you can get your hands on, but you won't see real change until you hit the gym. No one else can do your meditation for you.

Stress does not take a day off in your life. You must keep up these healthy meditation practices to stay healthy in your day-to-day life.

Because of this, you never want to take a day off for your meditation practice. When your life permits, meditate two or three times a day for a few minutes each time. For example, if meditating 30 minutes at a time is too much, do three 10-minute sessions per day; once in the morning when you wake up, once at noon before lunch, and once just before you go to bed.

This is the number one biggest mistake that new meditators make, never getting around to starting their practice. It's easy to make up problems that prevent you from meditating, but the reality is that one solution exists: To get started now.

Falling Asleep

Often, the only spare moments we have for meditation are late at night, close to when we're going to bed. You try as best as you can to meditate but quickly find instead that you've fallen asleep. This can be annoying and frustrating that you do not see results from what you're doing, especially when it's hard to see another way to go about it.

If you end up going to sleep while you meditate, consider it a good sign of positive and healthy behavior. It's never good to get mad at yourself. Instead, take it as a sign that something is going right. It is normal for you to fall asleep since you're tired after the day's work. Instead of being mad, be glad that you were able to fall asleep without stress.

Even just a few meditation techniques and focusing on the chakras before sleep is a good start. The following day, you can then wake up and pick up, meditating where you left off. And this time, you'll be able to meditate successfully, allowing you to feel relaxed and giving you the tools to face the day.

Failing to Prepare Your Meditation Environment

Once you have established a routine for your daily meditation practice, you should focus your attention on creating a good environment to make daily practice easier. You might wonder what this means for you. At the minimum, you should focus on the following:

Set aside a place in your home where you can meditate freely. This space should be quiet, and you should only use it for meditation or other spiritual practices if possible.

You'll want to find something like a cushion or mat to help you sit in your meditation area. Setting aside a chair for this purpose is good too.

Place a stopwatch or another convenient time-telling device where it isn't too distracting.

All of these steps are very important. It's quite likely that when you first resolve yourself to begin meditation that you will be feeling highly inspired, but this won't likely last for very much time. However, when you have a meditation environment already established, it will become easier for you to keep a consistent routine even during these "uninspired" periods. When everything is already arranged, there's a great chance that you'll see the area ready to go, sit down and begin meditating.

Forcing Yourself

If you're trying to meditate while in a noisy place or you have trouble focusing your mind on one thing, sitting in silence for meditation is both taxing and aggravating. If that sounds like a situation you're often in, it's best to accept it.

But, how is it possible to focus when you're surrounded by noise? The best thing to do is pick a sound close to you that can hold your interest and focus on it. The longer you focus on this sound, the more that it will help your meditation.

The best way to do this is to be aware of the noise and bring your attention to it. The more practice you have with this, the easier it will be to find yourself at ease in any noisy situation and still meditate. You might think that this can't be done, but it's possible. When you become a more experienced practitioner of meditation, you learn how to block out the sounds around you and integrate them into your meditation.

So you shouldn't think that you can't practice meditating because you're away from home. Practice doing it anywhere where you have the chance.

The next time you think you're going to fall off the meditation wagon, try practicing it a little, even while you're on public transportation.

It becomes easier for you to do this with practice. Once you get the hang of meditating where you are, when you do this, it helps you with reducing a variety of negative mental ailments and even improve pain tolerance.

Failing to Set a Daily Time for Meditation

Setting a clearly defined time for your meditation day after day is an important factor in getting you trained to be consistent with your routine. While it's useful to meditate anywhere, it's best to stick to a time for consistency's sake. Our recommendation is for this time to be early in the morning before daily life gets too distracting.

Setting too High Expectations for Yourself

It can be a disaster for you to set expectations that are too high when you're still beginning on your journey of learning how to meditate. Like anything else in life, at some points, you'll end up frustrated and disappointed.

Meditation is not simply something you do. It's a way of life. It will become easier for you as you do it more often and consistently over a long period.

You can expect this sort of process to see noticeable but gradual and incremental benefits. Certainly, you're going to notice more positive effects from meditation the longer you do it and the more consistent you are with it. You want to keep your expectations balanced as you begin your meditation journey.

What you'll come to find is that although you may not see the benefits of chakra meditation immediately, when you look back and reflect, it's easier to see how your well-being has improved.

Giving up Too Easily

Just sitting and meditating on your chakras can be difficult, especially when you're not used to it. So it is entirely understandable that you may have trouble developing the state of mind for effective meditation. All of us starting struggle and struggle, and there is no shame in that. The only failure you can make is for you to give up and not get back up the next day and attempt again. If you just keep going, you'll find that your mental aptitude will grow. It has no choice. Exercising will lead to greater results in time. So, don't judge yourself harshly, and just remember always to keep going.

Remember that the key here is a daily practice. You need to establish a routine first to allow meditation to work for you.

You Think Meditation Means Sitting like a Monk

You've probably seen an image of a monk meditating in a crossed-leg position. Perhaps you may have thought that all meditation was like this. This is not true, however. You can meditate in any position you like, especially while sitting down.

If you like sitting cross-legged, then, by all means, do so. However, if that doesn't work as well for you, then you should simply sit as you would normally, making sure not to lean. The important thing is that you sit in a way that allows you to be comfortable.

The trick is meditating consistently regardless of what position you decide to use. As you become more experienced, you may decide to see what you think about the cross-legged position. Most people who have not become accustomed to sitting in this position before are not very comfortable at first but often get better with practice.

Meditating Only When You Feel Like Everything Is Going Well

You want to be sure that you make meditation a habit, not something you do everyone once in a while. It's tempting to only turn to meditation during the times you feel down. But doing so can inhibit your progress in mastering your chakras.

Truthfully, meditation is often more effective when you're feeling good. This way, you can establish your well-being and balance your chakras effectively so that you're ready if life takes a turn.

All things considered, meditation is probably the most important tool we have to balance our chakras. The following steps shouldn't be used to replace meditation but to supplement it.

Here's a reminder on some of the best ways you can make meditation work for you:

- Set aside just a little time each day to build the habit of meditation.

- Find a peaceful place where you won't be disturbed for the duration of your meditation session. You want to make sure that this place is calm and quiet.

- Sit comfortably on the floor, folding your legs in front of you. Feel free to use a cushion if you would find the position uncomfortable otherwise. You'll want to stand up straight and allow your hands to fall limp on your knees.

- Start out by sitting for a few minutes in silence. You want to breathe deeply and evenly. It's important to clear your mind of negative emotions, especially anger and worry. These will interfere with your meditation and the chakra healing process.

- Close your eyes. This makes it easier for you to begin your visualizations.

- Run through all seven chakras during this process, visualizing the energy for each one.

Chapter 15: Meditation for Kundalini Energy

Kundalini Meditation

You can use this meditation to awaken your Kundalini energy and empower yourself to drop into your center for a balancing experience.

How to Use This Meditation

This awakening meditation should be used at least once per day. Using it first thing in the morning is a great way to awaken your Kundalini energy for the day. It also allows you to balance your energies as you go on, allowing you to continue operating from a gentle and intentional life force flow.

This meditation requires a specific breathing pattern which will be outlined in the script below. As you use this breathing alongside the reflection in your daily practice, you will likely find that the new breathing rhythm becomes your natural breathing rhythm. As this happens, you can be sure that you are effectively infusing your daily life with Kundalini energy. As the energy is at work, this renewed breathing pattern will infuse naturally.

This meditation, as previously mentioned, should take approximately 15 minutes. It is easy to incorporate into your daily routine and can have a powerful effect on all that you do. It will help you destress, awaken, and powerfully approach your day.

You must realize that Kundalini awakening and meditation are both journeys. As such, you need to commit to using these practices daily. This does not mean that you should feel shame or guilt if you miss a day. However, you want to do your best to refrain from missing any days. A truly awakened Kundalini energy will support you in remaining true to your practice day in and day out, which will allow you to continue to awaken your energy further. The more you commit, the more power you will gain from this practice.

The Meditation

Begin by finding your center. You can do this by bringing your awareness to the tip of your nose and then drop it straight down into the center of your body, where your solar plexus chakra resides. Once you have, begin using your breath as your center of focus. You want to block out the chatter in your mind by focusing entirely on rhythmic breathing. Right now is a great time to breathe deeply into your diaphragm, fill your lungs, and then fill your throat with air. As you exhale, empty your throat, then your lungs, and then your diaphragm. Continue doing this without pausing in between. Simply breathe. While you cannot ask your heart to beat at a different rate, breathing steadily in rhythmic breathing can help calm your heart center and bring your body into complete alignment and harmony.

As you continue breathing, begin breathing at a comfortable rate of four counts in… one, two, three, and four, and four counts out. one, two, three, and four. Keep this comfortable rhythm gently flowing through your lungs as you continue to keep your awareness on your center and your breath.

While you breathe, you may begin to recognize the movement in your lower belly area. This signifies that it is time to awaken your energy. This movement is often noticed as a sensation or a fluttering of energy. You can recognize it by the way it feels and keep your awareness of yourself and your inner world.

When you do, continue breathing with your count of four. Let the energy begin to arise, coming up your spine. This rising energy comes from your sacral chakra and continues to flow up your spine, purifying it with life force energy. Rather than visualizing it, simply become aware of the process as it happens. Stay focused on the energy rising, and set the intention to draw it up to your spine. Continue letting it rise until it reaches the crown of your head.

Breathe here for a few moments. In, two, three, four… out, two, three, four.

And as the process completes itself, take a few moments to relax and settle into the sensations that come with it. Then, when you are ready, draw your awareness back to the room and awaken yourself to the life around you. Take a few moments to feel how the sensation continues to reside within you, despite the fact that you are now awakened to the energy of the room. Carry this energy with you throughout your day, allowing it to be infused with all that you do. Let it inspire you, guide you, and continue to awaken you as you move throughout your daily routines."

Tantra Meditation

Tantra is another great practice to use to awaken Kundalini energy. If you have never heard of or used tantra before, you may be fascinated to learn more about it. Tantra is largely based on sexual life-giving energy and its ability to infuse the body with awakened energies. To truly understand the magic of tantra and how it can help you with your Kundalini awakening, we will further explore it. In case you do not yet know what tantra truly is or feel unfamiliar with the entirety of how it serves, we will begin by exploring a bit about tantra itself first. Tantra is an ancient, powerful, and secret spiritual technique from India. The word tantra has emerged from an Indian language, "Sanskrit" which consists of two root words: "Tan" which means Body, "Tra" which means a Process to Expand.

In Tantra, the body is used as a means for spiritual enlightenment. Unlike other spiritual techniques that consider the body filthy, tantra considers the body as a divine temple. Tantra uses sex as a tool for enhancing awareness and consciousness. Tantra merges yoga and sex to reach a new dimension. This new dimension is very deep and subtle that a human mind could ever imagine. In tantra, the practitioner performs several experiments within the human body. Experience, observations, and outcome of these systematic experiments reveal the truth about existence. This truth, when known to the ignorant mind, results in the attainment of liberation. Tanta is a way to merge body, mind, and energy to reach a higher consciousness level. Sex is an important instrument that is used in Tantra. This instrument, when used with full awareness, leads to awakening. Tantra is a profound meditation that eliminates all the boundaries of body and mind. It removes all the inner blockages. It relaxes the body, opens the heart, and brings the mind into focus. Tantra is not an ordinary casual technique that you want to do for sexual needs and bodily fulfillment. It is a spiritual practice where you awaken your core and merge your entire being in it. Tantra is a journey of human energy from base to infinite.

About Tantra

Tantra is a ritualistic spiritual practice that is rooted in Hinduism and Buddhism. This mystical text dates back as far as the 6th to 13th centuries. Many people hear the word tantra and immediately believe it is about sex. While it does incorporate sexual energies, it is done in a very intentional and ritualistic way to have a specific set of benefits for those using the practice. Tantra, however, has been highly sexualized by the Western culture since its introduction in the 19th century.

Though tantra does incorporate sexual energy, it uses the body as a tool to awaken spiritual energies. This happens through a complex series of rituals, chanting, and transcending.

How Tantra Affects Kundalini

Despite being harmless, Western society has often regarded Kundalini as highly sexual energy. Some people even believe it is rooted in sexual practices and that it may be taboo or bad. This is, however, a cultural bias granted by North Americans who approached the subject with a non-liberal perspective of sexual pleasure.

Kundalini yoga is considered to be a tantric practice itself. Through the chanting of specific sacred words, hand mudras, and intentional yoga poses, it awakens tantric energy to encourage Kundalini energy's awakening.

Kundalini incorporates tantra as a way of using the body as a tool to achieve liberation. The idea is that, when they are not awakened, our bodies can be tense and tight, often restricting the flow of Kundalini energy. However, our bodies are liberated when we awaken and tend to experience a greater sense of relaxation, pure energy flow, and peace.

The Practice of Tantra for Kundalini Awakening

When done properly, tantra in Kundalini awakening should only be practiced with a guru who is extremely powerful and who has mastered the teacher's inner state. These tantric gurus practice specific yoga practices with you in sequences that require two people to fulfill the yoga pose. This is highly responsible for awakening the Kundalini energies.

Tantric yoga practices for Kundalini awakening are not that different from traditional Kundalini yoga. The primary difference is that they incorporate another being. Because both beings become so energetically charged and awakened during the process, it is extremely powerful. Traditionally and ideally, this practice is accomplished between a man and a woman. This allowed for a balanced introduction of masculine and feminine energies, which ultimately creates the entire outcome.

That being said, tantric Kundalini yoga cannot be practiced on your own and should not be practiced without a guru. The energetic awakening power can be extremely intense and can result in nearly crippling experiences for many. This does not mean Kundalini energy is negative or bad, but it does mean that the experiences you can have due to the powerful energy can be difficult.

Pranayama Meditation

The Kundalini rises, and the chakras are located along the Sushumna Nadi. The Sushumna Nadi, physically located in the spinal cord, is a major prana channel, or breath energy, through the body. But in addition to the Sushumna Nadi there are many other major nadi, and in addition to those, more minor nadi than could be counted. Many of these nadi gather or originate in the Kama, a location very near the Muldahara chakra, where the Kundalini rests. The chakras can only be awakened if prana is flowing well and purposefully along with this entire system of nadis.

Our physical awareness of prana is in the form of breath. To balance the nadi and promote the flow of prana through them, allowing the chakras to awaken and Kundalini to rise, pranayama, or disciplined breathing exercises, are key. Pranayama helps to regulate the nadis and prana. It should be done diligently, but not to the point of exhaustion or discomfort. Typically, it's done first thing in the morning and holding an asana (described below).

There are many different practices in Pranayama, and to do it fully and gain benefits from it requires the help of a guru. To even begin requires extensive reading, at the very least. Many pranayama exercises involve balancing the flow of prana across the different sides of the body, through practices as simple as inhaling slowly through one nostril and exhaling out the other, more challenging exercises like holding the breath as long as possible and then exhaling silently through one nostril, and very advanced practices that involve taking air into the stomach.

Inner Vision Meditation

This meditation will require you to use your inner vision. Your words carry a vibration, and this imagery that you will picture will carry vibrations as well. You can use any type of image that brings up your energy. Test out a few images to see which will bring you sensations of hope, joy, and peace. To help you out, you can try imagining warm and golden sunlight. As you go through this mediation, your inner vision will likely start to show you things other than what we will discuss. This is perfectly fine as long as it is uplifting.

Find a comfortable and quiet place where you can be undisturbed for a while. Close your eyes and take a moment to scan through your body to see if anything is uncomfortable. Take some time to get adjusted into a comfortable and supported position.

Turn your attention to your breath, but don't try to change it. You may still notice that it changes on its own. It could become slower and deeper. It could also become faster. Don't worry about what it's doing. Allow it to be. All you need to do is watch your breath and be fully aware of how it feels to breathe in and breathe out.

If your mind starts to wander during your meditation, bring it back to your breath. Don't get upset, just return to your breath and how good it feels. Allow your breathing to relax you.

Now that you're relaxed and focused on your breathing picture yourself standing under the rays of a healing and warm golden light. This is a light of complete awareness. This is the essence of you and the essence of all living beings. It's all-encompassing love. It is the purest form of love. It is brighter than anything you have ever witnessed. It shines more than a million diamonds.

Allow this light to flow into your head and spread through your body at its will. Open yourself to the love that the light brings into you. It has your best interests in mind and is clearing out whatever is keeping you from your truth and love. As this light spreads through you, it fills your tissues, organs, cells, and every part of your body. It spreads into your memories and thoughts and fills them with healing. It will allow you to learn from what you have experienced.

This golden light pours through your crown chakra. It spreads into your third eye and opens up your connection to truth.

This warm and healing light flows down into your neck and through your throat chakra, balancing its energy and awakening your freedom. It spills over your shoulder and flows down into your arms and into your wrists, hands, and fingers. It shoots through the ends of your fingers and flows back into the earth.

From your fifth chakra, the light slides down into your heart and fills you with love. It pools in your heart and flows out in every direction. It continues to travel down your chest, front, and back.

The light fills up your solar plexus and fills up your rib cage. This area touches on your memories from your childhood and adolescents and your experiences with parental figures. They are all made new and are provided love, softness, and space. You now know that a Divine Companion accompanied you in everything that you did. This could be a Guardian Angel, Jesus, Buddha, and Love, whatever you choose. This Presence has always been with you and still is with you through all of your challenges.

This light continues to fill every fiber of your being and all of your thoughts as it spills down into your sacral chakra. It embraces the child that is still living in you. The light tells your inner child that he or she is loved for who he or she is. Your inner child is told that he or she hasn't done anything wrong. They only dreamed the things they did. Your inner child is beautiful, whole, and complete. They are loved and safe.

The golden light continues to travel down into your root chakra and spills in all directions. The light opens up your awareness of your connections with the love of family and other people on Earth. This light is awakening your wisdom.

The light heals everything it touches. Everything in your body is being filled with the love of this light. The light flows down your legs and exits your feet, flowing into the Earth.

You are now filled with the flow of this pure light from the top of your head through the tips of your toes. Everything is being rinsed in this golden light on every level. Anything that doesn't serve you is being removed, leaving behind a warm and loving feeling. Relax and allow everything to be released.

Stay in this moment for five minutes or more.

As you are with this light, sense that you are the light. Notice as your body dissolves into the light. Notice the freedom you feel of the light. You are unlimited and unbounded. Your creativity is unlimited because you are the light. You can do everything. You travel in every direction and are one with all beings.

Asana

Asana is what we typically think of when we think of yoga. As such, there are hundreds of them, and the proper way to practice them is widely documented and easy to learn. While the details of asana are unnecessary to document here, it is important to understand their specific relationship to Kundalini awakening.

Pranayama is only helpful when it's practiced in the position of an asana. Asana helps to focus the mind by controlling the body and promotes the physical health and circulation necessary for the prana to move freely and the Kundalini to awaken. This bodily focus helps control physical attachments and discomfort that create worldly troubles and make

Kundalini awakening impossible. However, for Kundalini awakening, certain poses are more helpful than others. Simple poses like the lotus position and similar sitting poses are beneficial, and the topsy-turvy and all-members pose, which involve balancing on the head and shoulders, respectively.

Asana is one of the best places to start in the journey toward Kundalini awakening. They lay the groundwork that prepares the body and mind. However, to get the proper benefit from them, they shouldn't be performed as a simple exercise. Practice regularly every day, and strive to keep the mind clear and focused on the body's actions. You'll be able to hold the poses for longer and longer, not merely because your body is becoming more flexible, but also because the mind gains the habit of becoming quiet, still, and patient—free from the passing thoughts and material wants that prevent spiritual awakening.

Transcendental Meditation

Think of yourself as a channel for energy to flow into and fill your body. As a receiver of energy, you must put aside your worries, ego, and thoughts. Think of yourself as a mere hollow capsule. You are an open doorway, a place for the energy in the universe to flow through. You will have an easier time achieving a relaxing, peaceful state if you start each meditation with these beliefs.

Leave thoughts of earthly concerns behind when you enter your holy place. You are no longer on Earth. You are traveling to a higher plane of consciousness. You should do this whether you are practicing by yourself or doing a reading for someone else. You will learn to practice advanced psychic techniques that will allow you to accomplish any goal you may have in mind. Whether it is reading one's emotions, viewing another place on Earth or this universe, receiving messages from another world or time, or locating a lost object, you must always begin with a centering meditation.

The Sacred OM Mantra Meditation

It is hard to nail down a single definition for the mantra because mantras have different meanings in different cultures around the world. Some mantras are used to create deeper relaxation during meditation, while others (like those used for tantra meditation) are considered sacred. Some mantras are based on musical measurements, while others are basic sounds that must be chanted or hummed.

It seems that the best general definition for a mantra is words or sounds that create certain qualities in the mind, with the intent of gaining certain benefits. For the purpose of mantras associated with the third eye, the mantras used should deepen the meditation and heighten the activation of the third eye. You can also use the mantras to close the third eye or invoke a certain nature, as discussed in the previous section.

Something so rooted in history that is still practiced day must produce some benefits. Otherwise, people would not still be using mantras after all this time. The research shows that there are several ways that mantras work to evoke certain qualities in the mind. On a spiritual level, many meditation masters say that the reason mantras work is because of the vibration. Mantras used during meditation involve grunts and hums; essentially, sounds that vibrate from deep within. These vibrations move through your being, affecting the frequency and vibrations of the molecules in your body. It makes molecular changes that, when paired with meditation and clear intentions, create the results that you experience in your body.

The auditory sense has evolved over time, and science shows that this evolution has created certain constants that affect our perception of the world. It is a combination of syllables, grunts, and pitches that come together to form language. This can be seen in humans as well as animals. Think about the way that dolphins or birds communicate with each other. Echoes are another example of this—think about the way a ball sounds bouncing off an empty basketball auditorium. The reverberation and the echoes create a sound that is unique to the ball and the court.

The reason that mantras are so effective at creating these changes in the body is that they are onomatopoetic. This simply means that you can hear the sound that the words make when they are being said, like a giggle, honk or crash. Sanskrit is a language that is created of onomatopoetic words. As most mantras, at least the classics, are derived from Sanskrit, you can hear the echoes of nature and the world around you. This creates the vibrational energy that brings about the desired effects.

As you mutter mantras, it creates physical events in the body and mind because of the primordial sounds. This is often said to be the echoes of nature traveling through the body and mind. Your intention also has a lot to do with the effects that are created. When you say a mantra, you are expecting a specific result. This is your intention. The utterance of your intention places the idea in your mind and creates the effects. Your consciousness then becomes intertwined with the mantra and its effects, and in this way, you are creating an echo that will produce your effects. Your entire being is now affected by your utterance of the mantra.

The Four Koshas (levels) of the Mantra

Mantras have four levels, each of them with a different intensity. When you first practice mantras, you may not experience the same effects that someone who knows how to increase the intensity would. You will still get some benefit from the mantra, but you will not experience its full benefit unless you deepen the intensity.

The four levels are of mantras are referred to as koshas. They include literal meaning, feeling, inner awareness, and soundless sound. The surface level is literal meaning. During this stage, the meaning of the mantra is understood, but not on a conscious level. Rather, it is experienced as a basic word. Next is the feeling, which is also subtle. However, it resembles feeling the meaning of the mantra. At the inner awareness kosha, you experience the inward feeling of the mantra. This is where it starts to make those molecular changes, and it deepens the experience of the word. The final stage is the soundless sound. This is where you will experience the most profound effects from the mantra. It reverberates inward and changes our consciousness completely, letting us become the mantra that we are uttering.

The goal when you meditate should be to move through all four levels. As you deepen the intention and continue to meditate, the mantra should deepen in meaning, and you should start to feel it internally.

Opening the third eye is all about potential and possibilities. It is about awakening the mind to a higher level of perception and letting our mind analyze the minute details that we overlook. It is about having a certain openness toward the third eye, making your mind receptive to the information that it is sending you.

The most common sound that has been associated with meditation mantras, particularly meditation to induce a state of awareness and enlightenment is the sound 'OM'. The Om sound is pronounced with a long 'o', as 'Aum'. If you have ever seen Buddhist meditation, you probably have heard the sound, as it is traditionally used for opening the third eye.

Take a moment and create the sound with your mouth as you breathe. Your lips should be parted, and the sound should emanate from deep within you, seeming as though the vibration fills your whole being.

If there is one feeling that you could associate with this sound, it would be openness. Your mouth is open, and the sound is formless and empty. This gives it the ability to make your body open and formless, creating infinite possibilities in its molecular structure. A good way to think of the sound is as a gateway to becoming the sound that is created with the mantra. By making the 'Om' sound, you are opening the doorway to becoming this formless being with unlimited potential.

OM Chanting

The Om chant is often called the seed mantra, or the beej mantra. Ideally, you should sit straight up how you are comfortable, with your knees crossed 'Indian style'. Move away from any support, like walls or chairs. When you are ready, settle into the meditation by taking deep breaths and turning your attention to the pineal gland. Chant 'om' loudly, feeling the energy flow through you and the chakra opening. The energy will move through the third eye in a horizontal direction, branching out as far as you can see and merging with the infinite expanse of the universe and beyond.

Increase your volume and chant 'om' louder, Feel the energy of the sound you are making as it vibrates vertically, from the top of your head to the bottom of your toes and into the crust of the earth. Do the verbal chant twice more, then say Om mentally three times.

Continue to chant 'om' verbally and the mentally, as long as you would like. This should increase your focus as stress, anxiety, and fear all melt away. The 'om' chant is what is considered a charged mantra, meaning that it has its own energy. It resonates deeply and reaches into the third eye chakra, causing instant activation. Following the moment of activation, the circumference of the chakra grows, and the chant balances it. It is in this moment when you have the most potential to look inward or to look to a higher sense of realization. By combining this with traditional third eye meditation, the gateway to consciousness is open

The Gayatri Mantra

ॐ भूर् भुवः स्वः।
तत् सवितुर्वरेण्यं।
भर्गो देवस्य धीमहि।
धियो यो नः प्रचोदयात्॥

oṃ bhūr bhuvaḥ svaḥ
oṃ tat savitur vareṇyaṃ
bhargo devasya dhīmahi
dhiyo yo naḥ pracodayāt

Sanskrit transliteration:

Om bhūr bhuvah svah - tát savitúr váren(i)yam - bhárgo devásya dhīmahi - dhíyo yó nah prachodáyāt

Phonetic pronunciation:

Om bhoor bhu-wah swa-ha - tat savi-tur varen-yam - bhar-go de-va-sya dheem-a-hi - dhiyo yo nah pra-cho-day-at

" We meditate on the Spiritual Splendor of that Supreme and Divine reality, source of the physical, astral and celestial spheres of existence. Allow that divine being supreme to illuminate our intellect, so that we can realize the Supreme Truth."

Rig Veda, Gayatri Mantra

Conclusion

Awakening the Kundalini is a special opportunity that not everyone can do in his/her lifetime. Although it may be difficult, consider even the hardships as gifts that will make you a better person at many levels. Remember that other people like you have undergone the activation and have managed to overcome it —seek them and ask for help if you need to.

It is said that the Spirit has its reasons for doing things, and we humans are simply complying with its wishes. It communicates with us through synchronicities (meaningful coincidences), events, dreams, sudden insights, and much more. The more aligned we are with the Spirit, the more blessed we become. So, try your best to become more spiritual and listen to what the divine is trying to tell you.

Do not be troubled when you think you have "sinned" or that you are becoming less spiritual. The Spirit may have allowed you to move away from it to teach you valuable lessons. If you find the need to return, just do so without overly chastising yourself. Even if you are an enlightened individual, it never means that you must never commit mistakes.

The activated Kundalini represents our connection with the Divine. We can still be human if we want to, but we also gain the advantage of being Divine while still in our flesh. This is not an obligation but more of an experience for us to learn from and enjoy. So, take it easy, and do more of what you want if you truly desire it. You will be able to do more now.

The next step is to reaffirm every day that you are on your way to becoming a better, fuller you. Believe in yourself and your ability to make the changes necessary to realize your goals. Once you've removed the clutter from your mind, you will turn to overthink into focused achieving every day. You may have heard many times over, "easier said than done." Well, you should be excited to learn how to do what you set your mind to do. You've wanted to make a change for a long time. Taking steps to make your goals come to fruition is something many people never achieve.

Printed in Great Britain
by Amazon

13634563R00112